At Sylvan, we believe reading is one of life's most important, most personal, most meaningful skills and we're so glad you've taken this step to become a successful reader with us. We know spelling, vocabulary, and reading comprehension are all critical to successful, thoughtful, and rewarding reading. A strong foundation in reading prepares fourth-graders to continue to read to learn and makes them stronger readers and better learners.

At Sylvan, successful reading instruction encompasses numerous reading processes with research-based, developmentally appropriate, and highly motivating, entertaining, and thought-provoking lessons. The learning process relies on high standards and meaningful parental involvement. With success, students feel increasing confidence. With increasing confidence, students build even more success. It's a perfect cycle. That's why our Sylvan workbooks aren't like the others. We're laying out the roadmap for learning. The rest is in your hands.

Parents, you have a special role. While your child is working, stay within earshot. If he needs help or gets stuck, you can be there to get him on the right track. And you're always there with supportive encouragement and plenty of celebratory congratulations.

One of the best ways to see learning progress is to check one's own work. Each section of the workbook includes a Check It! strip. As your child completes the activities, he can check his answers with Check It! If he sees any errors, he can fix them himself.

At Sylvan, our goal is confident readers who have the skills to tackle anything they want to read. We love learning. We want all children to love it as well.

We hope you and your child enjoy *Sylvan 4th-Grade Super Reading Success*. As your child continues on his academic journey, your local Sylvan Learning Center can also partner with your family in ensuring your child remains a confident, successful, and independent learner! Turn the page for more information and a special offer on our in-center service.

The Sylvan Team

Sylvan Learning Center.
Unleash your child's potential here.

No matter how big or small the academic challenge, every child has the ability to learn. But sometimes children need help making it happen. Sylvan believes every child has the potential to do great things. And, we know better than anyone else how to tap into that academic potential so that a child's future really is full of possibilities. Sylvan Learning Center is the place where your child can build and master the learning skills needed to succeed and unlock the potential you know is there.

The proven, personalized approach of our in-center programs deliver unparalleled results that other supplemental education services simply can't match. Your child's achievements will be seen not only in test scores and report cards but outside the classroom as well. And when he starts achieving his full potential, everyone will know it. You will see a new level of confidence come through in everything he does and every interaction he has.

How can Sylvan's personalized in-center approach help your child unleash his potential?

• Starting with our exclusive Sylvan Skills Assessment®, we pinpoint your child's exact academic needs.

• Then we develop a customized learning plan designed to achieve your child's academic goals.

• Through our method of skill mastery, your child will not only learn and master every skill in his personalized plan, he will be truly motivated and inspired to achieve his full potential.

To get started, included with this Sylvan product purchase is $10 off our exclusive Sylvan Skills Assessment®. Simply use this coupon and contact your local Sylvan Learning Center to set up your appointment.

And to learn more about Sylvan and our innovative in-center programs, call 1-800-EDUCATE or visit www.educate.com. *With over 1,100 locations in North America, there is a Sylvan Learning Center near you!*

4th-Grade
Super Reading Success

Published in the United States by Random House, Inc., New York, and in Canada by Random House of Canada Limited, Toronto.

www.tutoring.sylvanlearning.com

Created by Smarterville Productions LLC
Cover and Interior Photos: Jonathan Pozniak
Cover and Interior Illustrations: Duendes del Sur

First Edition

ISBN: 978-0-375-43007-7

Library of Congress Cataloging-in-Publication Data available upon request.

This book is available at special discounts for bulk purchases for sales promotions or premiums. For more information, write to Special Markets/Premium Sales, 1745 Broadway, MD 6-2, New York, New York 10019 or e-mail specialmarkets@randomhouse.com.

PRINTED IN CHINA

10 9 8 7

Spelling Contents

Vocabulary Contents

Reading Comprehension Contents

Checking your answers is part of the learning.

Each section of the workbook begins with an easy-to-use Check It! strip.

1. Before beginning the activities, cut out the Check It! strip.

2. As you complete the activities on each page, check your answers.

3. If you find an error, you can correct it yourself.

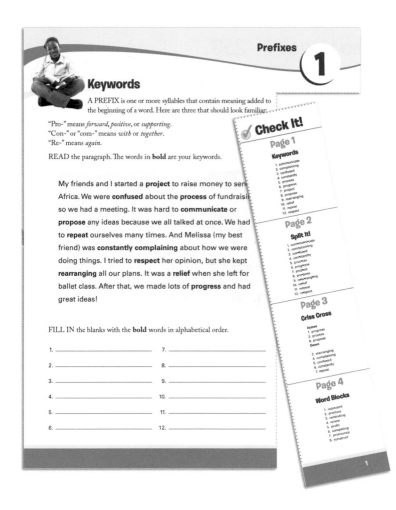

4th-Grade Spelling Success

Keywords

A PREFIX is one or more syllables that contain meaning added to the beginning of a word. Here are three that should look familiar:

"Pro-" means *forward*, *positive*, or *supporting*.
"Con-" or "com-" means *with* or *together*.
"Re-" means *again*.

READ the paragraph. The words in **bold** are your keywords.

My friends and I started a **project** to raise money to send to Africa. We were **confused** about the **process** of fundraising, so we had a meeting. It was hard to **communicate** or **propose** any ideas because we all talked at once. We had to **repeat** ourselves many times. And Melissa (my best friend) was **constantly complaining** about how we were doing things. I tried to **respect** her opinion, but she kept **rearranging** all our plans. It was a **relief** when she left for ballet class. After that, we made lots of **progress** and had great ideas!

FILL IN the blanks with the **bold** words in alphabetical order.

1. communicate
2. complaining
3. confusingly
4. constantly
5. progress
6. project
7. propose
8. process
9. repeat
10. respect
11. relief
12. rearranging

✓ Check It!

Page 1

Keywords

1. communicate
2. complaining
3. confused
4. constantly
5. process
6. progress
7. project
8. propose
9. rearranging
10. relief
11. repeat
12. respect

Page 2

Split It!

1. com•mu•ni•cate
2. com•plain•ing
3. con•fused
4. con•stant•ly
5. proc•ess
6. prog•ress
7. proj•ect
8. pro•pose
9. re•ar•rang•ing
10. re•lief
11. re•peat
12. re•spect

Page 3

Criss Cross

Across
1. progress
3. process
8. propose
Down

2. rearranging
4. complaining
5. confused
6. constantly
7. repeat

Page 4

Word Blocks

1. represent
2. produce
3. reminding
4. renew
5. profit
6. competing
7. pronounce
8. construct

✓ Check It!

Page 5

Word Search

Page 6

Match Up

1. e
2. b
3. g
4. f
5. i
6. h
7. a
8. c
9. d

Split It!

SPLIT these keywords into syllables, using dots to mark the breaks.

HINT: A prefix is usually its own syllable. Also, when a syllable ends in a LONG vowel sound, it usually ends with a vowel, like this: *pa•per*.

TIP: You usually use "com-" when the next letter is "p," "m," or "b."

Example: control   con•trol

communicate	1.	Com•mu•ni•cate
complaining	2.	com•plai•ning
confused	3.	con•fused
constantly	4.	Consonantly
process	5.	Pro•cess
progress	6.	pro•gress
project	7.	Pro•Ject
propose	8.	Pro•Pose
rearranging	9.	rea•rrans•ins
relief	10.	re•lief
repeat	11.	re•peat
respect	12.	re•spect.

Criss Cross

FILL IN the grid by answering the clues with keywords.

ACROSS

1. Improvement

3. Method or system

8. Suggest an idea

DOWN

2. Putting things in a different order

4. Whining

5. Puzzled

6. Something that never stops is done…

7. To say again

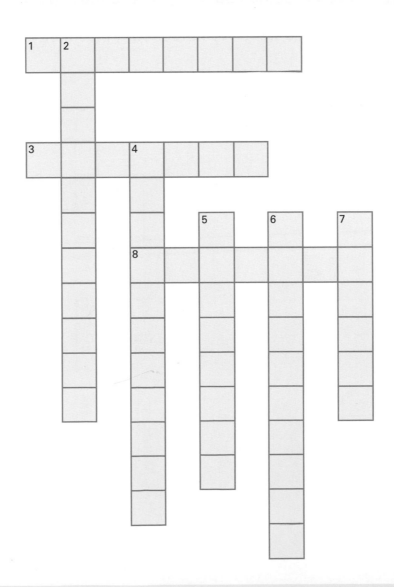

Word Blocks

FILL IN the blanks with "<u>com</u>" or "<u>con</u>," "<u>re</u>," or "<u>pro</u>" to make the correct word. Then FILL IN the word blocks with words of the same shape.

Example: That show is a <u>repeat</u>. I've seen it before!

I went to the library to ____new the books I haven't finished yet.

The candy costs us $1 and we sell it for $2. That's a dollar ____fit!

My art class is working together to ____struct a tower out of toothpicks.

How do you ____nounce the word *anemone*?

We sent Jeremiah to the coach so he could ____present the team.

With a little help, I can ____duce ten chocolate cream pies a day!

Our tennis team is ____peting in a major tournament.

Thanks for ____minding me about the sneaker sale!

Word Search

FILL IN the blanks with "com" or "con," "re," or "pro" to make the correct word. Then CIRCLE the words in the word grid. Words go down and across, not diagonally or backwards.

Example: It's a <u>relief</u> to drop my heavy backpack!

1. I broke Mrs. Arora's window and had to pay to get it ____paired.

2. All the band members have their names listed in the ____gram.

3. That house isn't made of brick. It's made of ____crete blocks.

4. It's hard to ____pare Superman with Batman. They're very different.

5. My brother and I are staging a ____test against broccoli. Join us!

6. The YMCA will ____vide towels if you want to swim.

7. Mickey won the burping ____test again. He's the best burper in town.

8. My sister is in love with her college history ____fessor. Yuck!

9. It took me two weeks to ____cover from the flu.

10. My parents are trying to ____vince me to clean the garage. Yeah, right.

W	P	M	C	Z	R	K	P	P	E	R
C	R	X	O	W	E	C	R	R	X	E
O	O	P	M	C	L	O	U	O	R	P
N	G	R	P	O	I	N	C	T	E	A
V	R	O	A	N	E	T	L	E	C	I
I	A	P	R	O	F	E	S	S	O	R
N	M	F	E	R	E	S	W	T	V	E
C	O	N	C	R	E	T	E	B	E	D
E	Q	P	R	O	V	I	D	E	R	P

Match Up

Here are some words that share the same ROOT, or body, but have different prefixes. MATCH the word on the left with the definition on the right. WRITE the letter of the answer in the blank.

Example: composition   putting things (like words) together in a certain way

1. reposition ____

2. retest   ____

3. protest   ____

4. contest   ____

5. confuse   ____

6. refuse   ____

7. contract   ____

8. retract   ____

9. protract   ____

a.   an agreement between people

b.   to test again

c.   to take back

d.   make longer, draw out

e.   to put in a different place

f.   a competition

g.   to disagree

h.   garbage (or to say *no*)

i.   to puzzle or cause doubt

 **Check It!**

Cut out the Check It! section on page 1, and see if you got the answers right.

Keywords

Did you know that there are lots of prefixes that mean *not*? Here are a few:

"non-" as in *nonfat*

"in-" and "im-" as in *incorrect* and *impossible*

"dis-" as in *disagree*

READ the paragraph. The words in **bold** are your keywords.

It's very **immature** to act badly on an airplane. Kicking the seat in front of you is totally **impolite**. And you shouldn't be **disrespectful** of the flight attendants or **disobey** their orders. They **disapprove** of that kind of **nonsense**. Last time I flew, I only brought one **nonfiction** book to read. Luckily, it was a **nonstop** flight. An **indirect** flight, with stops along the way, would have been **inexpensive**, but also **inconvenient** and longer. I was **impatient** to be on the ground again!

FILL IN the blanks with the **bold** words in alphabetical order.

1. _____

2. _____

3. _____

4. _____

5. _____

6. _____

7. _____

8. _____

9. _____

10. _____

11. _____

12. _____

Check It!

Page 7

Keywords

1. disapprove
2. disobey
3. disrespectful
4. immature
5. impatient
6. impolite
7. inconvenient
8. indirect
9. inexpensive
10. nonfiction
11. nonsense
12. nonstop

Page 8

Stack Up

2-Syllable Words
1. nonsense
2. nonstop

4-Syllable Words
1. inexpensive
2. disrespectful
3. inconvenient

3-Syllable Words
1. impatient
2. immature
3. disobey
4. nonfiction
5. Indirect
6. disapprove
7. impolite

Page 9

Word Search

```
N O N F I C T I O N
E X P E N S I V E O
N D A Z D W M U M N
O I T D I S D P X S
N S M R V I O Y Y E
S O E W E K S L Q N
T B N D C Y X I I S
O E T R T N T T M E
P Y M A T U R E U N
C O N V E N I E N T
```

Page 10

Spotlight on "Un-"

1. unwilling
2. undecided
3. unfamiliar
4. unpopular
5. unemployed
6. unripe
7. ungrateful
8. unimportant
9. unpleasant
10. unnatural

Bonus:
1. uncomfortable
2. discomfort
3. unarmed
4. disarm

✓ Check It!

Page 11

Pick the One!

1. nonbeliever
2. imperfect
3. inactive
4. nonmember
5. uncertain
6. disappear
7. impure
8. unauthorized
9. nonexistent
10. impractical
11. indefinite
12. nontoxic
13. inhuman
14. disapproving
15. impersonal
16. unfamiliar
17. dishonest
18. unlimited
19. insane
20. unseen
21. insincere
22. unscientific
23. nonswimmer
24. unwelcome

Page 12

Split It!

1. dis•o•bey
2. dis•re•spect
3. dis•ap•prove
4. im•ma•ture
5. im•pa•tient
6. im•per•son•al
7. in•con•ven•ient
8. in•di•rect
9. in•ex•pen•sive
10. in•for•mal
11. in•hu•man
12. non•fic•tion
13. non•prof•it
14. non•sense
15. un•bro•ken

Stack Up

READ the keywords out loud. SORT them by the number of syllables.
FILL IN the blanks with the sorted words.

TIP: Use the "im-" prefix with words that start with "m" or "p."

impatient	immature	disobey	nonfiction
inexpensive	nonsense	indirect	disapprove
disrespectful	inconvenient	nonstop	impolite

2-Syllable Words
Example: nonfat

1. _____

2. _____

4-Syllable Words
Example: impossible

1. _____

2. _____

3. _____

3-Syllable Words
Example: incorrect

1. _____

2. _____

3. _____

4. _____

5. _____

6. _____

7. _____

Word Search

FILL IN the blanks with keywords and their opposites. Then CIRCLE the words underlined in blue in the word grid. Words go down and across, not diagonally or backwards.

Example: If <u>polite</u> means being nice, then <u>impolite</u> means being rude.

1. If _____ means *costly,* then _____ means *cheap.*

2. If _____ means *willing to wait,* then _____ means *unable to wait.*

3. If _____ means *straightforward,* then _____ means *not straightforward.*

4. If _____ is *a story that isn't true,* then _____ is *a true story.*

5. If _____ means *grownup,* then _____ means *childish.*

6. If _____ means *easy,* then _____ means *difficult.*

7. If _____ means *to take a break,* then _____ means *to keep going.*

8. If _____ means *to follow orders,* then _____ means *to break the rules.*

9. If _____ means *intelligence,* then _____ is *silliness.*

N	O	N	F	I	C	T	I	O	N
E	X	P	E	N	S	I	V	E	O
N	D	A	Z	D	W	M	U	M	N
O	I	T	D	I	S	D	P	X	S
N	S	I	M	R	V	I	O	Y	E
S	O	E	W	E	K	S	L	Q	N
T	B	N	D	C	Y	X	I	I	S
O	E	T	R	T	N	T	T	M	E
P	Y	M	A	T	U	R	E	U	N
C	O	N	V	E	N	I	E	N	T

Spotlight on "Un-"

Guess what? There's another prefix that means *not*. ADD the prefix "un-" to each new word. FILL IN the blanks with the right "un-" word.

civilized	decided	employed	familiar	grateful	important
natural	pleasant	popular	ripe	welcome	willing

1. Chad will not shower no matter what. He's totally _____.

2. Vicki hasn't chosen a skirt yet. She's still _____.

3. I've never been on this block before. It's _____.

4. Someone with zero friends is very _____.

5. Don't have a job? Then you're _____.

6. A fruit that's not ready to eat is _____.

7. If you can't say, "thank you," then you're _____.

8. A clean shirt is _____ to me, but my mom feels differently.

9. Aunt Trudy thinks the Crawfords are _____ because they're loud.

10. A baby duck with three heads? That's _____!

Bonus

There are times when "dis-" and "un-" share a word. FILL IN the blank with "dis-" or "un-" to make the right word.

1. This hard chair is _____comfortable.

2. My _____comfort is caused by this hard chair.

3. That man has no weapons, so he is _____armed.

4. If he had weapons and you took them away, you would _____arm him.

Pick the One!

CIRCLE the word that uses the right prefix.

Not a believer	1. inbeliever	nonbeliever
Not perfect	2. inperfect	imperfect
Not active	3. inactive	imactive
Not a member	4. unmember	nonmember
Not certain	5. uncertain	incertain
Not appearing anymore	6. disappearing	unappearing
Not pure	7. inpure	impure
Not authorized	8. inauthorized	unauthorized
Not existent	9. inexistent	nonexistent
Not practical	10. inpractical	impractical
Not definite	11. indefinite	imdefinite
Not toxic	12. untoxic	nontoxic
Not human	13. inhuman	dishuman
Not approving	14. disapproving	inapproving
Not personal	15. nonpersonal	impersonal
Not familiar	16. infamiliar	unfamiliar
Not honest	17. dishonest	unhonest
Not limited	18. dislimited	unlimited
Not sane	19. insane	nonsane
Not seen	20. unseen	nonseen
Not sincere	21. insincere	imsincere
Not scientific	22. inscientific	unscientific
Not a swimmer	23. inswimmer	nonswimmer
Not welcome	24. unwelcome	diswelcome

Split It!

SPLIT these words into syllables, using dots to mark the breaks.

HINT: A prefix is usually its own syllable.

Example: incorrect   in•cor•rect

disobey	1. _____
disrespect	2. _____
disapprove	3. _____
immature	4. _____
impatient	5. _____
impersonal	6. _____
inconvenient	7. _____
indirect	8. _____
inexpensive	9. _____
informal	10. _____
inhuman	11. _____
nonfiction	12. _____
nonprofit	13. _____
nonsense	14. _____
unbroken	15. _____

Check It!

Cut out the Check It! section on page 7, and see if you got the answers right.

Keywords

Here are a few more prefixes for your brain to chew on:

"Fore-" means *before* or *in front*, as in *foresee*.
"En-" or "em-" means *in*, *on*, or *to make*, as in *enrage*.

READ the paragraph. The words in **bold** are your keywords.

> The weather **forecast** called for rain, so we went to the museum. In the **foreground** of one painting, there was a man with his hands on his **forehead** and a ring on his **forefinger**. He was **enclosed** in a cage and he looked really angry. The painting was **entitled** "**Enraged** Man **Entrapped** in Cage." I learned that the artist was **unemployed** when he painted this. But it **empowered** his career, making him the **foremost** artist of his time and **enriching** him beyond his wildest dreams!

FILL IN the blanks with the **bold** words in alphabetical order.

1. _____   7. _____

2. _____   8. _____

3. _____   9. _____

4. _____   10. _____

5. _____   11. _____

6. _____   12. _____

✓ Check It!

Page 17

Pick the One!

1. enlarge
2. embrace
3. foresee
4. entrust
5. employ
6. preheat
7. endanger
8. forethought
9. empower
10. preexist
11. foreman
12. prearrange
13. encircle

Page 18

Blank Out!

1. entangle
2. forewarned
3. revision
4. encourage
5. premature
6. profile
7. nonsmoking
8. dissatisified
9. insecure
10. discourage
11. disorder
12. contribute

Split It!

SPLIT these keywords into syllables, using dots to mark the breaks.

HINT: A prefix (or a suffix) is usually its own syllable.

TIP: Use the "em-" prefix with words that start with "b" or "p."

employ	1. _____
empower	2. _____
enclose	3. _____
enrage	4. _____
enrich	5. _____
entitle	6. _____
entrap	7. _____
forecast	8. _____
forefinger	9. _____
foreground	10. _____
forehead	11. _____
foremost	12. _____

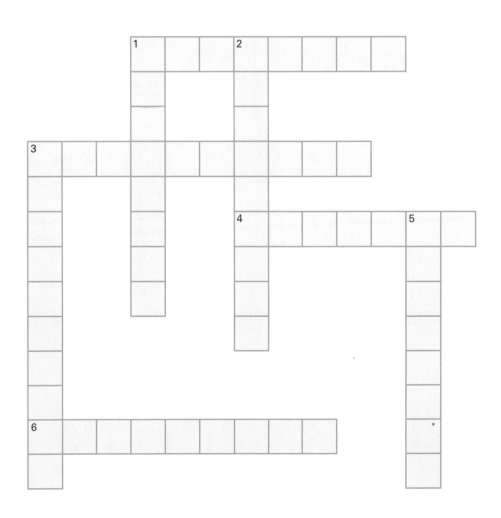

Criss Cross

FILL IN the grid by answering the clues with keywords.

ACROSS

1. The very first

3. The front part of a picture, closest to you

4. Put in a rage

6. Making rich

DOWN

1. The front of your head

2. Made more powerful

3. Your front finger

5. Made or gave a title

Word Blocks

Don't forget the prefix "pre-," which, like "fore-," means *before* or *first*.

FILL IN the blanks with either "fore" or "pre" to make the correct word. Then, FILL IN the word blocks with words of the same shape. Be sure to include the prefix.

Example: The label says to precook the meat first.

My sister has a scar on the front part of her arm, her _____ arm.

Arnold's Dad got us tickets to a _____ view of the next Disney movie.

Kids who are too young for kindergarten go to _____ school.

When an animal has four legs, the front ones are called the _____ legs.

As a _____ caution, make sure you have your cell phone.

When you buy movie tickets online, you have to _____ pay.

Pick the One!

CIRCLE the word that uses the correct prefix.

Example: To put in code (encode) *emcode*

Make large	1. enlarge	emlarge
Enclose in your arms	2. enbrace	embrace
See something before it happens	3. foresee	presee
Put your trust in	4. entrust	emtrust
Make use of, to hire	5. enploy	employ
Heat up beforehand	6. foreheat	preheat
Put in danger	7. endanger	emdanger
A thought beforehand	8. forethought	prethought
Make more powerful	9. enpower	empower
Exist before	10. foreexist	preexist
The lead man on a job	11. foreman	preman
Arrange ahead of time	12. forearrange	prearrange
Put in a circle	13. encircle	emcircle

More Prefixes

Blank Out!

Here are the prefixes we've covered so far: "con-," "pro-," "re-," "in-," "non-," "dis-," "un-," "fore-," "en-," and "pre-" Let's try them out on new words!

warned	secure	order	courage	vision	file
mature	satisfied	tribute	smoking	tangle	

FILL IN the blanks by adding a prefix to one of the words in the box.

HINT: *Courage* is used twice.

Example: Don't drink the water here. It's totally impure.

1. Clumsy Kristy managed to _____ herself in the jump rope!

2. The smell of smoke _____ me of the fire.

3. My story wasn't funny enough, so I wrote a _____.

4. I was afraid to sing in the play, but Mom smiled to _____ me.

5. Since Ziggy's only 12, driving lessons would be _____ for him.

6. MTV played a _____ of my favorite band that had lots of information.

7. My parents always ask for a _____ room at a hotel.

8. When I miss a goal, I can tell Coach Cruz is _____.

9. Maria isn't sure about her voice, so she's _____ about singing on stage.

10. If Thom keeps losing tennis matches, it'll _____ him from playing.

11. While the men were painting, our house was in total _____.

12. Mom says everyone has to _____ to cleaning the house.

✓ Check It!

Cut out the Check It! section on page 13, and see if you got the answers right.

18

Keywords

We've got three shiny new prefixes to play with!

"Over-" means *too much* or *above*.
"Under-" means *below*, *lower*, or *too little*.
"Inter-" means *among*, *between*, or *together*.

READ the paragraph. The words in **bold** are your keywords.

> I stayed **overnight** at my friend Cal's. He lives near the **interstate** highway. His little brother wore nothing but purple **underpants** and a shirt that said: "**Overworked** and **Underpaid**." His older brother refused to **interact** with us; he was watching a basketball game that had gone into **overtime**. Pepper, Cal's little sister, kept **interrupting** our conversation to show us stuff on the **Internet**. Dinner was completely **undercooked** and gross. Later, we tried to use Cal's new telescope, but the sky was **overcast**. I knew I wouldn't **oversleep** the next morning. I was ready to leave!

FILL IN the blanks with the **bold** words in alphabetical order.

1. _____
2. _____
3. _____
4. _____
5. _____
6. _____
7. _____
8. _____
9. _____
10. _____
11. _____
12. _____

Split It!

SPLIT the keywords into syllables, using dots to mark the breaks.

HINT: Here's how to split the prefixes: o•ver   un•der   in•ter

Example: understand   un•der•stand

interact

Internet

interrupt

interstate

overcast

overnight

oversleep

overtime

overworked

undercooked

underpaid

underpants

1. _____

2. _____

3. _____

4. _____

5. _____

6. _____

7. _____

8. _____

9. _____

10. _____

11. _____

12. _____

Word Search

FILL IN the blanks with keywords. Then CIRCLE the words in the word grid.
Words go down and across, not diagonally or backwards.

1. My brother gets paid extra when he works _____.

2. Dad made me clean the garage all day! I'm totally _____.

3. The old lady next door lives alone and doesn't _____ with anybody.

4. My computer's got a really fast _____ connection.

5. Are these beans _____ or are they supposed to be frozen?

6. Tyrell has a loud alarm clock so he won't _____.

7. In my dream, I was walking down the street in just my _____!

8. Sunny days are too hot! I like when the sky's a little _____.

9. Don't _____ me! Let me finish my speech!

10. Zella only gets $3 an hour? She's really _____.

X	I	O	V	E	R	T	I	M	E	Q	N	R
U	N	D	E	R	C	O	O	K	E	D	I	I
N	T	O	O	V	R	V	U	N	D	I	N	T
D	E	V	U	N	D	E	R	P	A	N	T	S
E	R	E	O	V	E	R	W	O	R	K	E	D
R	A	R	I	N	T	S	Y	I	M	E	R	Y
P	C	C	U	N	D	L	P	A	N	X	N	I
A	T	A	L	R	W	E	O	O	F	B	E	N
I	F	S	I	N	T	E	R	R	U	P	T	T
D	G	T	O	V	E	P	X	Q	V	R	C	W

Spotlight on "Sub-"

"Sub-" is another prefix that means *under* or *less than*.

READ each sentence. UNSCRAMBLE the **bold** word. FILL IN the blanks with the unscrambled words.

HINT: All of the words start with the prefix "sub-" or "under-."

I always **reeduniln** my name when I sign notes.

If you had a **serabimun**, you could go deep under the ocean.

Walt wants to build an **wretunerda** city. He likes fish!

To join the club, you have to **tumbis** a form online.

Garrett put stickers on the **sidderune** of his skateboard.

We took the **wabusy** to the Central Park Zoo.

The **buttelis** of this book is *A True Story*.

We live in a **rubbus** of Chicago.

We get **bezrous** temperatures here every winter!

Dad wears an **thirsderun** beneath his fancy shirts.

Don't talk about frogs! That's a forbidden **jebcust**.

The train goes **gerruddounn** through a tunnel.

Lydia doesn't like me. She treats me like I'm **baushnum**.

Mom will **cattrubs** a dollar from my allowance if I skip a chore.

1. _____

2. _____

3. _____

4. _____

5. _____

6. _____

7. _____

8. _____

9. _____

10. _____

11. _____

12. _____

13. _____

14. _____

Pick the One!

CIRCLE the word with the correct prefix.

Not weighing enough	1. subweight	underweight
Involving two or more nations	2. undernational	international
Below ground	3. underground	interground
On the other side of the ocean	4. overseas	underseas
A ship that goes deep under water	5. undermarine	submarine
A line beneath some words	6. overline	underline
Translate between languages	7. overterpret	interpret
Too full	8. overloaded	underloaded
Divide into smaller parts	9. underdivide	subdivide
Eat too much	10. overeat	intereat
Below the water	11. underwater	interwater
A town outside a city	12 interurb	suburb
Dressed too formally	13. overdressed	underdressed
The bottom side	14. overside	underside
Where two streets come together	15. subsection	intersection
A coat you wear on top of your clothes	16. overcoat	undercoat
Less than normal	17. undernormal	subnormal
To get in the middle	18. underfere	interfere
Where a street crosses above another street	19. overpass	underpass
Do too much	20. overdo	underdo

Prefixes Everywhere!

Stack Up

SORT the words in the box into the categories. FILL IN the blanks with the sorted words, including the prefixes.

HINT: Some words can be used with more than one prefix. Say each word with each prefix. Does it sound right?

face	ground	hear	load	look	marine	mission	national
rule	stand	taking	turn	title	total	water	

Words That Go with "Under-"
Example: underwear

1. _____

2. _____

3. _____

4. _____

Words That Go with "Over-"
Example: overweight

1. _____

2. _____

3. _____

4. _____

5. _____

6. _____

Words That Go with "Sub-"
Example: subway

1. _____

2. _____

3. _____

4. _____

Words That Go with "Inter-"
Example: internet

1. _____

2. _____

3. _____

✔ Check It!

Cut out Check It! to see if you got the answers right.

Keywords

Do you have room for three more prefixes?

"Semi-" means *half* or *moderately*, like *semicircle*, which is half of a circle.
"Anti-" means *against* or *opposite*, like *antiwar*.
"Multi-" means *much* or *many*, like *multicolor*.

READ the paragraph. The words in **bold** are your keywords.

Uh-oh. Mom has her **semiannual** cold. She's taking **antibiotics** and a bunch of **multivitamins**. She sits on the couch all day, wrapped in a **multicolored** blanket, with a **multitude** of magazines and tissues in a **semicircle** in front of her. When I asked if I could watch the basketball **semifinals** in the living room, she said no. She gets so **antisocial** when she's sick! Meanwhile, Dad is writing an **antiwar** article for a **multinational** magazine. He's stinky, because he forgets to wear **antiperspirant**. All he thinks about are commas and **semicolons**. I'm living in a nuthouse!

FILL IN the blanks with the **bold** words in alphabetical order.

1. _____   7. _____
2. _____   8. _____
3. _____   9. _____
4. _____   10. _____
5. _____   11. _____
6. _____   12. _____

✓ Check It!

Page 29

Pick the One!

1. antifreeze
2. semitropical
3. misspelled
4. multicultural
5. antislavery
6. antiperspirant
7. semimonthly
8. mistyped
9. multipurpose
10. semisoft
11. misuse
12. semiprecious
13. multimedia
14. mismatched
15. semisolid
16. misunderstood
17. antidote
18. multiplies

Page 30

Author! Author!

Check to be sure you used six of the words. Then look them up in a dictionary to see if you used them correctly.

Split It!

SPLIT the keywords into syllables, using dots to mark the breaks.
HINT: Here's how to split the prefixes:

an•ti   mul•ti   sem•i

Example: multiply   mul•ti•ply

antibiotics

antiperspirant

antisocial

antiwar

multicolored

multinational

multitude

multivitamins

semiannual

semicircle

semicolons

semifinals

1. _____

2. _____

3. _____

4. _____

5. _____

6. _____

7. _____

8. _____

9. _____

10. _____

11. _____

12. _____

Criss Cross

FILL IN the grid by answering the clues with keywords.

ACROSS

2. Half comma, half colon

3. Has many colors

4. Of many countries

5. Prevents sweaty armpits

6. Drugs that fight infections

DOWN

1. Halfway through the finals

3. A pill containing many vitamins

Multiprefixed!

Word Blocks

Don't forget the prefix "mis-," which means *wrong*. It's easy to confuse it with "anti-," which means *against* or *opposite*.

FILL IN the blanks with either "anti" or "mis" to make the correct word.
Then FILL IN the word blocks with words of the same shape. Be sure to include the prefix.

Example: Why does everyone misspell my name?

Marsha's great-great-grandpa was part of the _____slavery movement.

The paper said I won the lottery, but that was a _____print!

We put _____freeze in the car to keep the engine going.

Our dog's former owner used to _____treat him.

You lost everything in a fire? That's a major _____fortune!

Where are my headphones? I must have _____placed them.

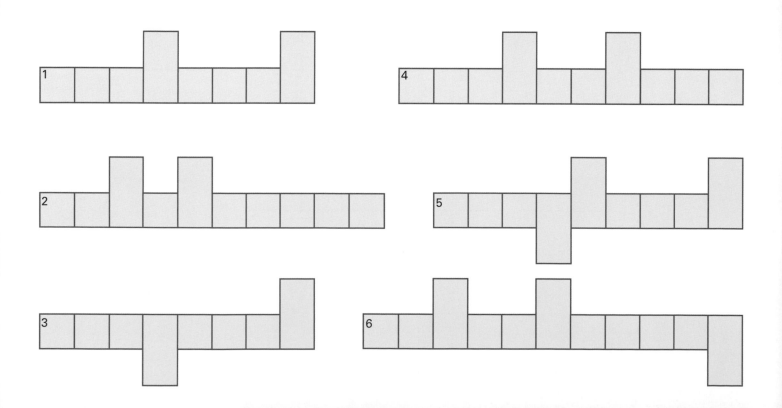

Pick the One!

CIRCLE the word with the correct prefix.

Keeps things from freezing	1. misfreeze	antifreeze
Moderately tropical	2. semitropical	multitropical
Spelled wrong	3. misspelled	antispelled
Of many cultures	4. semicultural	multicultural
Against slavery	5. multislavery	antislavery
Stops perspiration	6. misperspirant	antiperspirant
Twice a month	7. semimonthly	multimonthly
Typed wrong	8. semityped	mistyped
Has many purposes	9. semipurpose	multipurpose
Moderately soft	10. semisoft	multisoft
Put to the wrong use	11. misuse	semiuse
Moderately precious	12 semiprecious	misprecious
Uses many kinds of media	13. semimedia	multimedia
Matched incorrectly	14. mismatched	antimatched
Not quite solid	15. semisolid	antisolid
Understood the wrong thing	16. misunderstood	semiunderstood
Something that prevents poisoning	17. misdote	antidote
Makes many more	18. semiplies	multiplies

Author! Author!

It's your turn to do the writing. Use at least six of the new words to write a story, a poem, or a list of crazy sentences. Have fun!

insane	nonstop	disappear	imperfect	unpopular	forecast
prehistoric	enrich	embrace	overboard	underwear	submarine

_____

_____

_____

_____

_____

_____

_____

_____

_____

_____

_____

_____

_____

_____

 **Check It!**

Cut out Check It! to see if you got the answers right.

Spell Check

READ each sentence. CIRCLE the word that has the wrong prefix. FILL IN the blanks with the correct words. Use the right prefixes!

Example: Fluffy likes to ⟨underact⟩ with other dogs.   interact

1. I can be shy, so I feel unsecure at parties.

2. Cindy used my computer and misorganized my files.

3. It would be inpractical to fly. Let's take the train.

4. Mom left a note to commind me to bring my lunch.

5. Being captain would enpower you to set the batting order.

6. Check the weather precast before the picnic.

7. Don't indanger yourself by crossing against the light.

8. I'm at the undersection of 4th and Main. Where are you?

9. Ew! I saw Dad in his subpants today.

1. _____

2. _____

3. _____

4. _____

5. _____

6. _____

7. _____

8. _____

9. _____

✓ Check It!

Page 31

Spell Check

1. insecure
2. disorganized
3. impractical
4. remind
5. empower
6. forecast
7. endanger
8. intersection
9. underpants

Page 32

Criss Cross

ACROSS
4. semiannual
6. foreleg
7. protect

Down
1. misread
2. nonbeliever
3. multiracial
5. premature

Page 33

Word Blocks

1. incorrect
2. nontoxic
3. impatient
4. inaction
5. disagree
6. invisible
7. indirect
8. unnatural

Page 34

Stack Up

Compound Words	Words with Prefixes
1. bridesmaid	1. composition
2. courtroom	2. discontinue
3. everybody	3. forecast
4. gentleman	4. misplace
5. lightweight	5. proclaim
6. screwdriver	6. understand

Criss Cross

FILL IN each blank with the right prefix to finish the word.
WRITE the words in the grid.

ACROSS

4. Twice a year, our church has its _____annual bingo night.

6. The horse lost a shoe on her _____leg, not her back one.

7. Shira tries to _____tect her little sister from bullies.

DOWN

1. Kara _____read the flyer and went to the wrong store.

2. My parents are religious, but Grandpa is a _____believer.

3. My karate class is _____racial, with kids from all over.

5. It's _____

Word Blocks

ADD the correct prefix to make the opposite of the words listed. FILL IN the word blocks with the new words of the same shape.

HINT: Use one of the "not" prefixes: in-/im-, non-, dis-, or un-.

Example: willing   unwilling

action   _____

toxic   _____

direct   _____

agree   _____

visible   _____

correct   _____

natural   _____

patient   _____

Stack Up

A PREFIX is not usually a word by itself. A COMPOUND WORD is a word that's made of two words stuck together. Can you tell the difference?

SORT the words by category.

composition	bridesmaid	courtroom	discontinue
everybody	forecast	gentleman	lightweight
misplace	proclaim	screwdriver	understand

Compound Words	**Words with Prefixes**
Example: highway	*Example: misspell*

Compound Words

1. _____
2. _____
3. _____
4. _____
5. _____
6. _____

Words with Prefixes

1. _____
2. _____
3. _____
4. _____
5. _____
6. _____

 **Check It!**

Cut out Check It! to see if you got the answers right.

6

Keywords

A SUFFIX is an ending added to a word that changes its meaning. Here are a few for starters:

"-Y" turns *trick* (noun) to *tricky* (adjective).
"-Ly" turns *sad* (adjective) to *sadly* (adverb).
"-Er" and "-or" turn *act* (verb) to *actor* (noun).
"-Ness" turns *happy* (adjective) to *happiness* (noun).

READ the paragraph. The words in **bold** are your keywords.

In my family, I'm the **brainy** one, and my sister, Isabella, is the performer. She practices skating every **frosty** winter morning with an **instructor** at the rink in town. You may think that's **crazy**, but in competition, Isabelle defeats every **challenger** with **perfectly** executed moves that show the **thoroughness** of her training. Once we watched **anxiously** as she leaped into a triple axle. She landed it **flawlessly**! My sister's **seriousness** about ice skating keeps her really busy, which means a little **loneliness** for me. But that's okay. She says I can be her **manager** one day!

FILL IN the blanks with the **bold** words in alphabetical order.

1. _____
2. _____
3. _____
4. _____
5. _____
6. _____
7. _____
8. _____
9. _____
10. _____
11. _____
12. _____

Meet the Suffixes

✓ Check It!

Page 39
Spotlight

1. sorrowful
2. flawless
3. plentiful
4. doubtless
5. delightful
6. breathless
7. effortless
8. bountiful
9. humorless
10. disgraceful
11. restless
12. flavorful
13. weaponless
14. meaningful
15. worthless
16. scornful

Page 40
Alternate Endings Again!

1. po•lite•ness
2. kind•ness
3. home•less
4. cloud•less
5. good•ness
6. spot•less
7. sweet•ness
8. spine•less
9. fit•ness
10. care•less•ness
11. thought•ful•ness
12. cheer•less
13. pain•less•ness
14. hope•ful•ness
15. thought•less•ness
16. youth•ful•ness

Stack Up

READ the keywords out loud. SORT them into the categories.

anxiously   brainy   challenger   crazy

flawlessly   frosty   instructor   loneliness

manager   perfectly   seriousness   thoroughness

Nouns
Examples: sadness, teacher

1. _____
2. _____
3. _____
4. _____
5. _____
6. _____

Adverbs
Example: happily

1. _____
2. _____
3. _____

Adjectives
Example: tricky

1. _____
2. _____
3. _____

Alternate Endings

When a word ends in "y," change the "y" to an "i" before adding the suffix: *merry, merrily, merriness.*

ADD suffixes to these words to make them into adjectives and adverbs.

HINT: Change the "y" to an "i" before changing the adjectives into adverbs.

Example: trick   tricky   trickily

Noun	Adjective (+ "-y")	Adverb (+ "-ly")
itch	1. _____	_____
gloom	2. _____	_____
grump	3. _____	_____
mood	4. _____	_____
worth	5. _____	_____
frost	6. _____	_____
scratch	7. _____	_____

Bonus

When a word ends in "e," you usually drop the "e" before adding the "y" or "ly."

Example: bounce   bouncy   bouncily

Noun	Adjective	Adverb
breeze	1. _____	_____
slime	2. _____	_____
craze	3. _____	_____

Morph It!

Did you know that the suffix "-er" can turn a verb into a noun? Well, now you do. FILL IN the blanks by adding the suffix "-er" to make the **bold** verb into a noun.

TIP: When a word ends in one vowel followed by one consonant (like *bag*), you usually have to double the consonant before the suffix.

*Example: A person who **bags** groceries is a **bagger**.*

1. Mr. McDonald **preaches** sermons, so he's a _____.

2. On TV, Lizzie Winters does the noon **forecast**. She's a weather _____.

3. Theresa **babysits** her brother. She's a _____.

4. Ricky **entertains** us with his jokes. Someday, he'll be an _____.

5. My uncle **manages** a candy store. He's a store _____.

6. Michael **dresses** up Mom's hair for special nights. He's a hair_____.

7. Since Lucy is always **making** trouble, Mom calls her a trouble_____.

8. The tool you use to **drive** in a screw is a screw_____.

9. An act that **stops** the show is a show_____.

Bonus

Add "-or" to the **bold** words to make them into people.
HINT: If a verb ends in an "e," drop the "e" before you add the ending.

1. If you **protect** someone, you're his _____.

2. Ilia **instructs** me in Spanish. She's an _____.

3. Mr. Garbo **investigates** crime. He's an _____.

4. Wow, the person who **sculpted** that statue is a great _____.

Spotlight on "-Ful" and "-Less"

Here are two more suffixes that are really useful to know!

"-Ful" means full of, so *useful* means *full of use*.

"-Less" means lacking, so *useless* means *has no use*.

FILL IN the blanks to match the clues.

Example: Full of use   useful

Clue	
Full of sorrow	1. _____
Lacking any flaw	2. _____
Full of plenty	3. _____
Has no doubt	4. _____
Full of delight	5. _____
Lacking breath	6. _____
With no effort	7. _____
Full of bounty	8. _____
Has no humor	9. _____
Full of disgrace	10. _____
Not able to rest	11. _____
Full of flavor	12. _____
Has no weapon	13. _____
Full of meaning	14. _____
Lacking worth	15. _____
Full of scorn	16. _____

Alternate Endings Again!

ADD "-less" to the nouns to make them adjectives.
ADD "-ness" to the adjectives to make them nouns.
SPLIT the new words into syllables, using dots to mark the breaks.

HINT: A suffix is usually its own syllable. Some words have more than one suffix!

Example: joy   joy•less   useful   use•ful•ness

polite	1. _____
kind	2. _____
home	3. _____
cloud	4. _____
good	5. _____
spot	6. _____
sweet	7. _____
spine	8. _____
fit	9. _____
careless	10. _____
thoughtful	11. _____
cheer	12. _____
painless	13. _____
hopeful	14. _____
thoughtless	15. _____
youthful	16. _____

7

Keywords

You've seen how the suffixes "-er" and "-or" can turn a verb like *teach* into a noun like *teacher*. Here are two more suffixes that do the same thing!

"-Ment" turns *amaze* into *amazement*.

"-Ion" turns *act* into *action*.

READ the paragraph. The words in **bold** are your keywords.

Music is my life! I love to sing while my brother plays the **accompaniment** on his guitar. My **ambition** is to find **employment** as a musician. I could also give **instruction** to kids, write my own **composition** and **arrangement** of songs, and maybe even star in a musical **production**! My teacher has seen a lot of **improvement** in my work since I made the **commitment** to practice every day. Yesterday, I received an **invitation** to a major singing **competition**! I can barely handle the **excitement**!

FILL IN the blanks with the **bold** words in alphabetical order.

1. _____
2. _____
3. _____
4. _____
5. _____
6. _____
7. _____
8. _____
9. _____
10. _____
11. _____
12. _____

✓ **Check It!**

Page 41
Keywords
1. accompaniment
2. ambition
3. arrangement
4. commitment
5. competition
6. composition
7. employment
8. excitement
9. improvement
10. instruction
11. invitation
12. production

Page 42
Morph It!
1. accompaniment
2. arrangement
3. commitment
4. competition
5. composition
6. employment
7. excitement
8. improvement
9. instruction
10. invitation
11. production

Page 43
Alternate Endings
1. excitement
2. punishment
3. adoption
4. amusement
5. invention
6. retirement
7. treatment
8. prevention
9. settlement
10. management
11. reflection
12. replacement
13. advertisement
14. entertainment
15. arrangement
16. improvement
17. assignment
18. instruction

Page 44
Add It Up!
1. creation
2. civilization
3. judgment
4. confusion
5. starvation
6. competition
7. accompaniment
8. decision
9. permission
10. composition
11. decoration
12. relation
13. separation
14. argument
15. illustration
16. invitation

Total Suffixment!

 **Check It!**

Page 45

Alternate Endings

1. composer   composition
2. producer   production
3. protector   protection
4. settler   settlement
5. manager   management
6. mover   movement
7. employer   employment
8. illustrator   illustration
9. inventor   invention
10. arranger   arrangement

Page 46

Pick the One!

1. in•ven•tor
2. il•lus•tra•tion
3. ad•ver•tise•ment
4. com•po•si•tion
5. am•bi•tion
6. dec•o•ra•tion
7. ac•com•pa•ni•ment
8. com•pe•ti•tion
9. com•mit•ment
10. ar•range•ment
11. em•ploy•ment
12. ex•cite•ment
13. im•prove•ment
14. in•struc•tion
15. in•vi•ta•tion
16. pro•duc•tion

Morph It!

FILL IN the blanks with the noun version of each verb.

HINT: The answers are all keywords. The suffix "-ion" sometimes morphs into "-tion," "-ition," or "-ation."

Verb	Noun

Example: amaze   amazement

accompany   1. _____

arrange   2. _____

commit   3. _____

compete   4. _____

compose   5. _____

employ   6. _____

excite   7. _____

improve   8. _____

instruct   9. _____

invite   10. _____

produce   11. _____

42

Alternate Endings

ADD "ion" or "ment" to change the verbs into nouns. FILL IN the blanks with the new words.

Example: pay *pay<u>ment</u>* *subtract* *subtract<u>ion</u>*

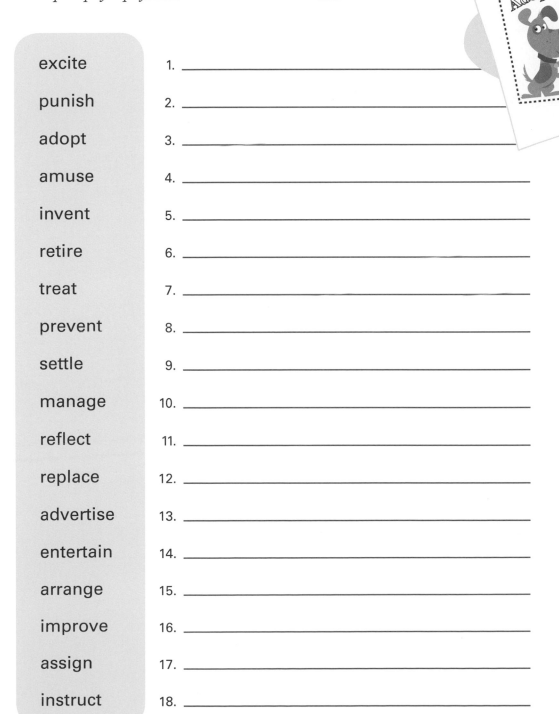

Adopt a Puppy Today

excite	1. _____
punish	2. _____
adopt	3. _____
amuse	4. _____
invent	5. _____
retire	6. _____
treat	7. _____
prevent	8. _____
settle	9. _____
manage	10. _____
reflect	11. _____
replace	12. _____
advertise	13. _____
entertain	14. _____
arrange	15. _____
improve	16. _____
assign	17. _____
instruct	18. _____

Add It Up!

Adding "ion" or "ment" can be tricky. Sometimes you have to drop or add letters to the word before you tack on the endings. Like when *add* becomes *addition*. Or when *divide* becomes *division*.

SOLVE the "problems" by adding the suffix.

HINT: Sometimes you'll add more than "ion" or "ment."

Verb   **Noun**

Example: (divide – de)   +   sion   =   division

(create – e) + ion   1. _____

(civilize – e) + ation   2. _____

(judge – e) + ment   3. _____

(confuse – e) + ion   4. _____

(starve – e) + ation   5. _____

(compete – e) + ition   6. _____

(accompany – y) + iment   7. _____

(decide – de) + sion   8. _____

(permit – t) + ssion   9. _____

(compose – e) + ition   10. _____

(decorate – e) + ion   11. _____

(relate – e) + ion   12. _____

(separate – e) +ion   13. _____

(argue – e) + ment   14. _____

(illustrate – e) + ion   15. _____

(invite – e) + ation   16. _____

Alternate Endings

ADD suffixes to these words to make them into people or other nouns.

HINT: If a verb ends in an "e," drop the "e" before adding the ending. Remember to watch for words that end in -tion, -ition, and -ation.

Verb	Person (+ "-er/-or")	Noun (+ "-ment/-ion")

Example: act   actor   action

Verb		
compose	1. _____	_____
produce	2. _____	_____
protect	3. _____	_____
settle	4. _____	_____
manage	5. _____	_____
move	6. _____	_____
employ	7. _____	_____
illustrate	8. _____	_____
invent	9. _____	_____
arrange	10. _____	_____

Total Suffixment!

Pick the One!

CIRCLE the correct syllable split for each word.

Example: management   ma•nage•ment   (man•age•ment)

inventor	1. in•vent•or	in•ven•tor
illustration	2. il•lus•tra•tion	ill•us•trat•ion
advertisement	3. ad•ver•tise•ment	ad•vert•ise•ment
composition	4. comp•o•sit•ion	com•po•si•tion
ambition	5. amb•i•tion	am•bi•tion
decoration	6. dec•o•ra•tion	de•co•rat•ion
accompaniment	7. acc•om•pa•nim•ent	ac•com•pa•ni•ment
competition	8. com•pe•ti•tion	comp•et•it•ion
commitment	9. com•mit•ment	comm•i•tment
arrangement	10. ar•range•ment	arr•ang•ement
employment	11. emp•loy•ment	em•ploy•ment
excitement	12. ex•ci•tement	ex•cite•ment
improvement	13. im•prove•ment	imp•ro•vement
instruction	14. inst•ruc•tion	in•struc•tion
invitation	15. in•vi•ta•tion	in•vit•at•ion
production	16. pro•duc•tion	pro•duct•ion

Keywords

You can make adjectives out of verbs, through the magic of the suffix like this:

"-Ive" turns *act* into *active*.
"-Able" turns *break* into *breakable*.

READ the paragraph. The words in **bold** are your keywords.

> Arnold is way too **competitive**. We play this **interactive** video game where you need to be really **creative** to win. Arnold's not usually a very **talkative** guy, but whenever I beat him, he starts calling me a cheater. He's so **excitable**! He says it's **unbelievable** that I could ever beat him fairly, even if my win was **decisive**. His anger is **uncontrollable**. After that, he gets **possessive** about the game console (it's his), and won't let me use it. That makes me **uncomfortable**, so I go home. His behavior is **unforgivable** and **inexcusable**!

FILL IN the blanks with the **bold** words in alphabetical order.

1. _____
2. _____
3. _____
4. _____
5. _____
6. _____
7. _____
8. _____
9. _____
10. _____
11. _____
12. _____

✓ Check It!

Page 47

Keywords

1. competitive
2. creative
3. decisive
4. excitable
5. inexcusable
6. interactive
7. possessive
8. talkative
9. unbelievable
10. uncomfortable
11. uncontrollable
12. unforgivable

Page 48

Morph It!

1. believable
2. comfortable
3. competitive
4. controllable
5. creative
6. decisive
7. excitable
8. excusable
9. forgivable
10. interactive
11. possessive
12. talkative

Page 49

Criss Cross

Across
1. excitable
3. unforgivable
4. possessive
5. talkative
7. believable
8. creative

Down
1. excusable
2. controllable
6. decisive

Page 50

Add It Up!

1. effective
2. inventive
3. employable
4. controllable
5. moveable
6. forcible
7. decisive
8. conceivable
9. arguable
10. adorable
11. sensible
12. agreeable
13. decorative
14. reversible
15. explainable
16. forgettable
17. explosive
18. imaginative

✓ Check It!

Page 51

Spell Check

1. effective
2. uncontrollable
3. moveable
4. reversible
5. instructive
6. inseparable
7. permissive
8. decorative
9. unforgettable
10. explosive
11. decisive
12. comfortable
13. unbelievable
14. agreeable

Page 52

Pick the One!

1. recognizable
2. submissive
3. treatable
4. talkative
5. separable
6. reversible
7. forcible
8. creative
9. excitable
10. controllable
11. explosive
12. huggable
13. inventive
14. interactive
15. effective
16. decisive
17. punishable
18. measurable

Morph It!

FILL IN the blanks with keywords to turn each verb into an adjective.

Some of the keywords are missing their "un-" or "in-" prefixes.

Verb	Adjective

Example: attract   attractive / wash   washable

believe	1. _____
comfort	2. _____
compete	3. _____
control	4. _____
create	5. _____
decide	6. _____
excite	7. _____
excuse	8. _____
forgive	9. _____
interact	10. _____
possess	11. _____
talk	12. _____

TIP: Sometimes, when a word ends in "e" (like *create*), you have to drop the "e" before adding the suffix. For example, *create*, *creative*. But other times, you keep the "e," like in *moveable*.

Criss Cross

FILL IN the grid by answering the clues.

ACROSS

1. Able to get very excited
3. Not able to be forgiven
4. Likes to possess things
5. Likes to talk a lot
7. Able to be believed
8. Good at creating things

DOWN

1. Able to be excused
2. Able to be controlled
6. Makes decisions easily

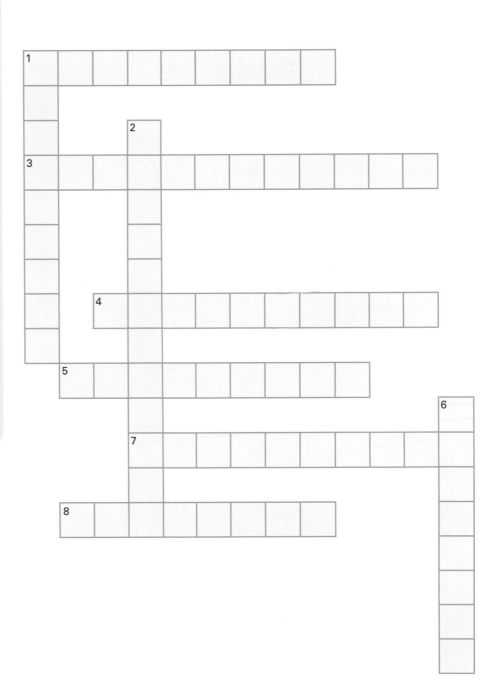

Add It Up!

SOLVE the "problems" by adding the suffixes.

Verb	Noun

Example: act + ive = active

effect + ive	1. _____
invent + ive	2. _____
employ + able	3. _____
control + l + able	4. _____
move + able	5. _____
(force – e) + ible	6. _____
(decide – de) + sive	7. _____
(conceive – e) + able	8. _____
(argue – e) + able	9. _____
(adore – e) + able	10. _____
(sense – e) + ible	11. _____
agree + able	12. _____
(decorate – e) + ive	13. _____
(reverse – e) + ible	14. _____
explain + able	15. _____
forget + t + able	16. _____
(explode – de) + sive	17. _____
(imagine – e) + ative	18. _____

Spell Check

READ each sentence. CIRCLE the word that has the wrong suffix.

FILL IN the blanks with those misspelled words. Use the right suffix and spell them right!

Example: My grandma is very (actable) for an old lady.   active

That stinky spray is pretty effectable at killing bugs.

1. _____

Ashley's curls are uncontrollative when it rains.

2. _____

Is this chair movible, or is it bolted down?

3. _____

This jacket is reversable. Turn it inside out and see!

4. _____

My last karate class was very instructable.

5. _____

Arthur and Veejay are best friends. They're inseparative!

6. _____

Katya's parents are very permittive.

7. _____

That pretty poster on your wall is very decorable.

8. _____

I'll remember our vacation forever. It was unforgettive.

9. _____

Dad's temper is very explodive. He's like a time bomb!

10. _____

Our team won a decidable victory that put us in the playoffs.

11. _____

Sit over here. That lumpy chair isn't very comfortive.

12. _____

Cecilia and Will are dating? That's unbelievible!

13. _____

Marcos and I never fight, because he's very agreeative.

14. _____

Pick the One!

CIRCLE the word in each row with the correct suffix.

Example: act (active) actable

recognize	1. recognitive	recognizable
submit	2. submissive	submittive
treat	3. treative	treatable
talk	4. talkable	talkative
separate	5. separable	separible
reverse	6. reversable	reversible
force	7. forcive	forcible
create	8. creative	createable
excite	9. excitable	excitive
control	10. controlable	controllable
explode	11. explodive	explosive
hug	12. hugable	huggable
invent	13. inventable	inventive
interact	14. interactive	interactible
effect	15. effective	effectible
decide	16. decidive	decisive
punish	17. punishable	punishive
measure	18. measureable	measurable

Keywords

Here are a couple of suffixes that usually make adjectives.

"-Al" or "-ial" means *about* or *having to do with*, like *bridal*, which means *having to do with the bride*.

"-Ous" or "-ious" means *full of* or *having*, like *joyous*, which means *full of joy*.

READ the paragraph. The words in **bold** are your keywords.

I was very **nervous** at my aunt's wedding. Since I was part of the **bridal** party, I had to walk down the aisle and wear a **formal** dress. Everyone was very **serious** during the ceremony, which included a short **memorial** to Grandma, who died last year. But the party afterward was completely **unceremonious**! People made **humorous** speeches and danced like crazy. My aunt is a very **social** lady with **numerous** friends. Her new husband is a wild, **adventurous**, **musical** guy. (He's in a **famous** band!) They make a great couple.

FILL IN the blanks with the **bold** words in alphabetical order.

1. _____
2. _____
3. _____
4. _____
5. _____
6. _____

7. _____
8. _____
9. _____
10. _____
11. _____
12. _____

✓ Check It!

Page 53

Keywords

1. adventurous
2. bridal
3. famous
4. formal
5. humorous
6. memorial
7. musical
8. nervous
9. numerous
10. serious
11. social
12. unceremonious

Page 54

Split It!

1. ad•ven•tur•ous
2. brid•al
3. fa•mous
4. for•mal
5. hu•mor•ous
6. me•mo•ri•al
7. mu•si•cal
8. nerv•ous
9. nu•mer•ous
10. se•ri•ous
11. so•cial
12. un•cer•e•mo•ni•ous

Page 55

Word Blocks

1. adventurous
2. famous
3. social
4. nervous
5. musical
6. unceremonious
7. bridal
8. humorous

Page 56

Spotlight

1. formal
2. royal
3. serious
4. ambitious
5. annual
6. enormous
7. special
8. fatal
9. funeral
10. loyal
11. moral
12. precious

✓ Check It!

Page 57

Add It Up!

1. official
2. spacious
3. virtuous
4. beneficial
5. glorious
6. criminal
7. suspicion
8. personal
9. mysterious
10. survival
11. colonial
12. original
13. racial
14. gracious
15. marvelous
16. skeletal

Page 58

Pick the One!

1. adventurous
2. memorial
3. digital
4. political
5. sacrificial
6. religious
7. magical
8. universal
9. nervous
10. autumnal
11. seasonal
12. social
13. rental
14. famous
15. natural
16. humorous
17. glacial
18. numerous
19. cultural
20. alphabetical

Split It!

SPLIT these keywords into syllables, using dots to mark the breaks.

Example: furious   *fu•ri•ous*

adventurous	1. _____
bridal	2. _____
famous	3. _____
formal	4. _____
humorous	5. _____
memorial	6. _____
musical	7. _____
nervous	8. _____
numerous	9. _____
serious	10. _____
social	11. _____
unceremonious	12. _____

54

Word Blocks

WRITE the keywords in the blanks. Then FILL IN the word blocks with keywords of the same shape.

Example: Full of fury   furious

Full of nerves _____

Having to do with society _____

Not full of ceremony _____

Full of adventure _____

Having to do with music _____

Having to do with the bride _____

Full of humor _____

Full of fame _____

1

2

3

4

5

6

7

8

Spotlight on Suffixes and Roots

Some words with prefixes or suffixes make sense right away, like *musical*. It's easy: music + -al = *musical*. But what about words like *special* or *serious*? "Spec" and "ser" aren't really words—they're word ROOTS. Sometimes the root is a clue to the meaning of a word.

| ambitious | annual | enormous | fatal | formal | loyal |
| moral | funeral | precious | royal | serious | special |

FILL IN the blanks with keywords..

1. Dad hates wearing a tuxedo for _____ dinners and dances.

2. Prince William is my favorite member of the _____ family.

3. Team practice is a very _____ occasion. No fooling around!

4. Taj is very _____. He wants to be president some day!

5. I only eat Aunt Bea's cookies once a year, at our _____ picnic.

6. Monster trucks have to be _____ so they can crush little cars.

7. Grandma is a very _____ lady.

   There's no one like her!

8. I can kill a video game alien with one

   _____ shot from my ray gun.

9. Mom and Dad were so sad after their

   friend's _____ .

10. Everyone in our family is a _____ Yankees fan. Go Yanks!

11. Our priest is always talking about _____ stuff, like being honest.

12. Uncle Jim gave his wife a necklace covered with _____ gems.

Add It Up!

SOLVE the "problems" by adding the suffixes.

Example: (fury – y) + ious = furious   *(bride – e) + al = bridal*

(office – e)	+	ial	1.	_____
(space – e)	+	ious	2.	_____
(virtue – e)	+	ous	3.	_____
(benefit – t)	+	cial	4.	_____
(glory – y)	+	ious	5.	_____
(crime – e)	+	inal	6.	_____
(suspect – ect)	+	icion	7.	_____
person	+	al	8.	_____
(mystery – y)	+	ious	9.	_____
(survive – e)	+	al	10.	_____
(colony – y)	+	ial	11.	_____
origin	+	al	12.	_____
(race – e)	+	ial	13.	_____
(grace – e)	+	ious	14.	_____
marvel	+	ous	15.	_____
(skeleton – on)	+	al	16.	_____

Pick the One!

CIRCLE the word in each row with the correct suffix.

Example: bride (bridal) brideous

adventure	1. adventural	adventurous
memory	2. memorial	memorous
digit	3. digital	digitous
politics	4. politicial	political
sacrifice	5. sacrificious	sacrificial
religion	6. religious	religial
magic	7. magicious	magical
universe	8. universal	universous
nerves	9. nervous	nerval
autumn	10. autumnus	autumnal
season	11. seasonous	seasonal
society	12. social	socious
rent	13. rental	rentious
fame	14. famous	famial
nature	15. naturous	natural
humor	16. humoral	humorous
glacier	17. glacous	glacial
number	18. numerous	numberal
culture	19. cultural	culturous
alphabet	20. alphabetous	alphabetical

Keywords

Our last suffixes can make verbs out of ordinary nouns like this:

"-Ize" means *to make*, like *capitalize*, which means *to make a capital letter*.
"-Ify" also means *to make*, like *beautify*, which means *to make something beautiful*.

READ the paragraph. The words in **bold** are your keywords.

> Yesterday, I helped Uncle Manny **organize** his tools, so he could **simplify** the way he stored them. While we worked, we **socialized** with Jed from next door. I tried to **memorize** all the different tools, but I found one I couldn't **identify**. It **mystified** me. Then I kicked over a jar of nails! Can you **visualize** the floor covered in sharp nails? I was **petrified**, afraid to move. Uncle Manny was **horrified** and **criticized** me angrily. I thought he'd have to be **hospitalized**! I quickly **apologized**, but it took an hour to find all the nails.

FILL IN the blanks with the **bold** words in alphabetical order.

1. _____
2. _____
3. _____
4. _____
5. _____
6. _____

7. _____
8. _____
9. _____
10. _____
11. _____
12. _____

✓ Check It!

Page 59

Keywords

1. apologized
2. criticized
3. horrified
4. hospitalized
5. identify
6. memorize
7. mystified
8. organize
9. petrified
10. simplify
11. socialized
12. visualize

Page 60

Morph it!

1. apologized
2. criticized
3. hospitalized
4. horrified
5. identify
6. memorize
7. mystified
8. simplify
9. socialize
10. visualize

Page 61

Alternate Endings

Verb	+ "-ing"	+ "-ed"
1. apologize	apologizing	apologized
2. hospitalize	hospitalizing	hospitalized
3. mystify	mystifying	mystified
4. memorize	memorizing	memorized
5. simplify	simplifying	simplified
6. visualize	visualizing	visualized
7. socialize	socializing	socialized
8. horrify	horrifying	horrified

Page 62

Add It Up!

1. magnetize
2. purify
3. finalize
4. summarize
5. alphabetize
6. energize
7. familiarize
8. glorify
9. humidify
10. colonize
11. civilize
12. personalize
13. fantasize
14. terrify
15. stabilize
16. justify

The Last Suffixes

✓ Check It!

Page 63
Spotlight

1. artistic	8. heroic
2. allergic	9. historic
3. athletic	10. idiotic
4. atmospheric	11. magnetic
5. climatic	12. majestic
6. comedic	13. melodic
7. economic	14. poetic

1. fantastic	fantastically
2. energetic	energetically
3. metallic	metallically
4. sympathetic	sympathetically
5. apologetic	apologetically

Page 64

Author! Author!

Check to be sure you used six of the words. Then look them up in a dictionary to see if you used them correctly.

Morph it!

FILL IN the blanks with the keyword verb that matches each noun.

HINT: Use the basic form of the verb with the "-ify" or "-ize" ending.

Example: beauty   beautify

apology	1. _____
critic	2. _____
hospital	3. _____
horror	4. _____
identity	5. _____
memory	6. _____
mystery	7. _____
simple	8. _____
social	9. _____
visual	10. _____

Alternate Endings

FILL IN the blanks with basic forms of the keywords. Then ADD the verb endings to make the different verb forms.

HINT: See the example for how to treat verbs that end in "y."

Example: Make beautiful   beautify   beautifying   beautified

Verb	Verb + "-ing"	Verb + "-ed"
Make an apology		
1. _____	_____	_____
Put in the hospital		
2. _____	_____	_____
Make a mystery		
3. _____	_____	_____
Put in your memory		
4. _____	_____	_____
Make more simple		
5. _____	_____	_____
Make visual		
6. _____	_____	_____
Be social		
7. _____	_____	_____
Make someone feel horror		
8. _____	_____	_____

Add It Up!

SOLVE the "problems" by adding the suffixes.

Example: (fury – y) + ious   = furious

magnet	+	ize	1. _____
(pure – e)	+	ify	2. _____
final	+	ize	3. _____
(summary – y)	+	ize	4. _____
alphabet	+	ize	5. _____
(energy – y)	+	ize	6. _____
familiar	+	ize	7. _____
(glory – y)	+	ify	8. _____
humid	+	ify	9. _____
(colony – y)	+	ize	10. _____
civil	+	ize	11. _____
personal	+	ize	12. _____
(fantasy – y)	+	ize	13. _____
(terror – or)	+	ify	14. _____
(stable – le)	+	ilize	15. _____
just	+	ify	16. _____

Spotlight on Just Add "-ic"

Suffixes are terrific! How about one more? When you add "-ic" to a verb like *terrify*, or to a noun like *angel*, voila! You get the adjectives *terrific* and *angelic*. Try it out!

ADD "-ic" to the words to turn them into adjectives.

HINT: If a word ends in an "e" or a "y," drop it!

Example: magnet   magnetic

artist	1. _____	hero	8. _____
allergy	2. _____	history	9. _____
athlete	3. _____	idiot	10. _____
atmosphere	4. _____	magnet	11. _____
climate	5. _____	majesty	12. _____
comedy	6. _____	melody	13. _____
economy	7. _____	poet	14. _____

Here are some tricky ones! Make these into both adjectives and adverbs.

HINT: To make an adverb from an adjective, just add a double suffix "-al" + "-ly" = "-ally."

	Adjective	**Adverb**
Example: drama + tic =	*dramatic*	*dramatically*

(fantasy – y) + tic	1. _____	_____
(energy – y) + etic	2. _____	_____
metal + lic	3. _____	_____
(sympathy – y) + etic	4. _____	_____
(apology – y) + etic	5. _____	_____

Author! Author!

It's your turn to do the writing. Use at least six of the words to write a story, a poem, or a list of crazy sentences. Have fun!

angelic	horrify	disagreeable	amusement
entertainer	uncontrollable	magnetic	unforgettable
flawless	apologize	invitation	interruption

_____

_____

_____

_____

_____

_____

_____

_____

_____

_____

_____

_____

_____

_____

Blank Out!

LOOK AT the clue. Then WRITE the matching suffix in each blank.

-y	-ful	-less	-ness	-er	-or	-ly	-ment
-ion	-ive	-able	-al	-ous	-ify	-ize	-ic

Means *full of*:

Means *lacking*:

Makes a verb:

Makes a verb into a noun:

Makes an adverb:

Makes a verb into a person:

Makes an adjective into a noun:

Makes a noun into an adjective:

Makes a verb into an adjective:

1. care___ ___ ___

2. care___ ___ ___

3. simpl___ ___ ___

4. magnet___ ___ ___

5. commit___ ___ ___

6. protect___ ___ ___

7. quick___ ___

8. instruct___ ___

9. teach___ ___

10. sweet___ ___ ___ ___

11. smell___

12. music___ ___

13. magnet___ ___

14. humor___ ___ ___

15. wash___ ___ ___ ___

16. possess___ ___ ___

✔ Check It!

Page 65
Blank Out!

1. careful
2. careless
3. simplify
4. magnetize
5. commitment
6. protection
7. quickly
8. instructor
9. teacher
10. sweetness
11. smelly
12. musical
13. magnetic
14. humorous
15. washable
16. possessive

Page 66
Pick the One!

1. reminder
2. simply
3. permissive
4. adeptness
5. central
6. horrific
7. purify
8. offensive
9. sincerely
10. preachy
11. critical
12. promptly
13. professor
14. constantly
15. penniless
16. illustrator
17. location
18. forgetfulness

Page 67
Morph It!

1. colonial
2. apologize, apologetically
3. criticize, critically
4. mystify, mysterious, mysteriously
5. energize, energetic, energetically
6. personalize, personally
7. magnetize, magnetic, magnetically
8. civilization, civilize, civilly
9. fantasize, fantastic
10. horrify, horrific, horrifically
11. instruction, instructively
12. agreeable, agreeably
13. excite, excitable, excitably
14. believer, believable, believably

Page 68
Word Search

F	E	O	V	E	R	C	O	O	K	E	D
U	M	L	E	S	I	W	V	G	K	U	I
N	P	Y	J	O	Y	F	U	L	U	N	S
D	O	U	B	T	L	E	S	S	N	T	A
E	W	U	W	L	O	B	L	E	S	A	B
R	R	E	N	D	E	A	N	T	I	U	L
W	E	N	O	S	H	A	R	M	F	U	L
I	U	N	S	X	Q	P	P	L	Y	E	U
G	Y	E	F	A	I	T	H	L	E	S	S
H	D	I	S	X	W	E	R	F	U	L	L
T	A	S	T	E	L	E	S	S	I	M	T

Pick the One!

CIRCLE the word with the correct suffix.

Example: Someone who acts is an   (actor)   *action*

Something that reminds you is a   1. reminder   remindment

To be simple, you do it   2. simply   simplely

If you permit things, you are   3. permittive   permissive

An adept person is known for   4. adeptment   adeptness

If it's in the center, it is   5. central   centrous

Something that horrifies you is   6. horrifious   horrific

To make something pure, you   7. purify   purifize

When you offend, you're being   8. offensive   offendify

To be sincere, you do it   9. sincerely   sincerious

If you preach a lot, you are   10. preachify   preachy

If you like to criticize, you are   11. critical   critious

To be prompt, you do it   12. promptious   promptly

Someone who professes is a   13. professor   professicator

To be constant, you do things   14. constantize   constantly

No pennies? Then you're   15. penniless   penniful

If you illustrate, then you're an   16. illustral   illustrator

You are located at your   17. location   locatement

A forgetful person suffers from   18. forgetion   forgetfulness

Morph It!

FILL IN the blanks by writing the correct form of the word.

	Noun	Verb	Adjective	Adverb
1.	colony	colonize	_____	colonially
2.	apology	_____	apologetic	_____
3.	critic	_____	critical	_____
4.	mystery	_____	_____	_____
5.	energy	_____	_____	_____
6.	person	_____	personal	_____
7.	magnet	_____	_____	_____
8.	_____	_____	civil	_____
9.	fantasy	_____	_____	fantastically
10.	horror	_____	_____	_____
11.	_____	instruct	instructive	_____
12.	agreement	agree	_____	_____
13.	excitement	_____	_____	_____
14.	_____	believe	_____	_____

Word Search

CHANGE the prefix or suffix to make the opposite of the words listed. FILL IN the blanks with the new words. Then CIRCLE the words in the word grid. Words go down and across, not diagonally or backwards.

overweight _____

tasteful _____

encourage _____

entangle _____

undercooked _____

overpower _____

enable _____

harmless _____

doubtful _____

faithful _____

joyless _____

F	E	O	V	E	R	C	O	O	K	E	D
U	M	L	E	S	I	W	V	G	K	U	I
N	P	Y	J	O	Y	F	U	L	U	N	S
D	O	U	B	T	L	E	S	S	N	T	A
E	W	U	W	L	O	B	L	E	S	A	B
R	E	N	D	E	A	N	T	I	U	N	L
W	R	D	I	S	C	O	U	R	A	G	E
E	N	O	S	H	A	R	M	F	U	L	U
I	U	N	S	X	Q	P	P	L	Y	E	N
G	Y	E	F	A	I	T	H	L	E	S	S
H	D	I	S	X	W	E	R	F	U	L	L
T	A	S	T	E	L	E	S	S	I	M	T

Keywords

When you have to spell a word you don't know, try to figure out its ROOT. What's a root? It's what's left when you take off the prefixes and suffixes.

Try these out:

Equalize comes from the root "equa" (also "equi") which means *equal*.
Scribble comes from the root "scrib" (also "script") which means *write*.

READ the paragraph. The words in **bold** are your keywords.

Hollywood, here I come! I **subscribe** to many movie magazines and **transcribe** scenes from my favorite films so I can practice them. My friend Sammy **describes** me as "a future movie star." He even asked me to **scribble** an **inscription** in his autograph album! He **equates** me with the star of his favorite TV show, and says I am **equally** talented. All I need is the right **script**! Mom thinks acting is **equivalent** to joining the circus and says I should go to the doctor and get a **prescription** for anti-Hollywood pills. Ha ha! Whether I'm singing or solving **equations** for math class, my talent shines all the way to the **equator**!

FILL IN the blanks with the **bold** words in alphabetical order.

1. _____
2. _____
3. _____
4. _____
5. _____
6. _____
7. _____
8. _____
9. _____
10. _____
11. _____
12. _____

 **Check It!**

Page 73

Split It!

1. de•scribe
2. e•qual•ize
3. eq•ui•ta•ble
4. e•qua•tion
5. e•qua•tor
6. e•qua•to•ri•al
7. e•qui•dis•tant
8. e•qui•nox
9. e•quiv•a•lent
10. in•scrip•tion
11. pre•scrip•tion
12. scrib•ble
13. sub•scribe
14. tran•scribe

Page 74

Morph It!

1. equalize, equally
2. equation, equitable
3. description
4. inscribe, inscribable
5. prescription, prescribable
6. subscription, subscribable
7. transcribe, transcribable

1. inequality
2. indescribable
3. unequal
4. resubscribe

Stack Up

SORT the keywords by their roots.

describes   equal   equates   equations

equator   equivalent   inscription   prescription

scribble   script   subscribe   transcribe

"Equi/Equa" Root
Example: equinox

1. _____

2. _____

3. _____

4. _____

5. _____

"Script/Scrib" Root
Example: unscripted

1. _____

2. _____

3. _____

4. _____

5. _____

6. _____

7. _____

Criss Cross

FILL IN the grid by answering the clues with keywords.

ACROSS

3. A written note from a doctor to the pharmacist

6. A longer way of saying equal

7. The written text of a play or movie

8. Math statements with equal signs

DOWN

1. Tells or writes how something looks

2. To write something down, or copy it

4. A written message in or on something

5. A line that divides the world into two equal halves

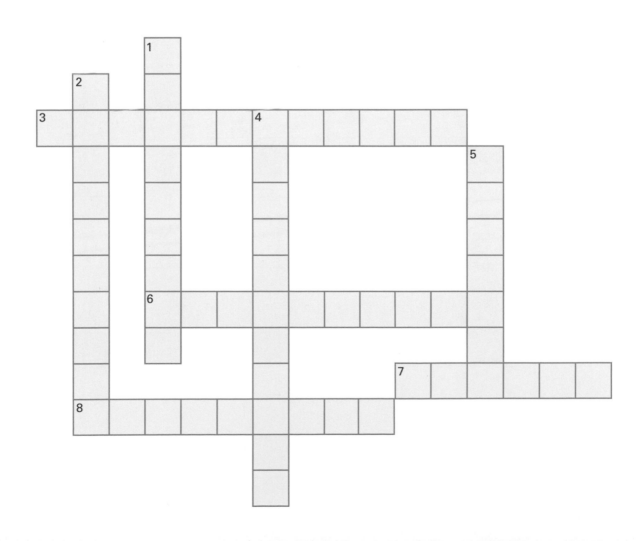

Word Blocks

CIRCLE the root "equi/equa" or "scrip/scrib" in each sentence. Then FILL IN the word blocks with the words of the same shape.

HINT: Use the whole word, not just the root!

For her birthday, I gave Mom a subscription to a gardening magazine.

When I had the flu, my doctor prescribed some antibiotics.

My house is equidistant from two comic book stores.

To practice typing, I make transcriptions of my favorite fairy tales.

There is serious inequality at camp, where the girls get the nicest cabins.

My brother gets a bigger allowance, so I asked Mom to equalize our allowances.

Day and night are the same length on the day of the equinox.

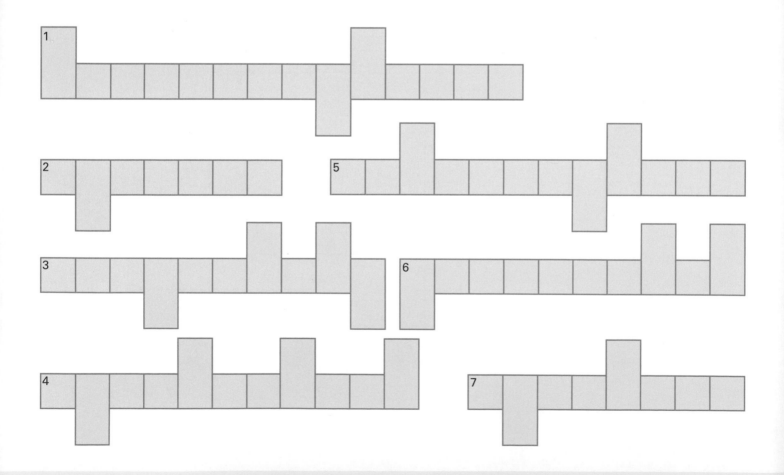

Split It!

SPLIT these words into syllables, using dots to mark the breaks.

HINT: Don't forget that syllables with short vowels usually end in a consonant.

Example: equal   e•qual

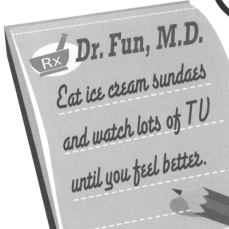

Rx Dr. Fun, M.D.
Eat ice cream sundaes and watch lots of TV until you feel better.

describe   1. _____

equalize   2. _____

equitable   3. _____

equation   4. _____

equator   5. _____

equatorial   6. _____

equidistant   7. _____

equinox   8. _____

equivalent   9. _____

inscription   10. _____

prescription   11. _____

scribble   12. _____

subscribe   13. _____

transcribe   14. _____

Morph It!

FILL IN the blanks by writing the correct form of the word.

	Noun	Verb	Adjective	Adverb
1.	equality	_____	equal	_____
2.	_____	equate	_____	equitably
3.	_____	describe	describable	
4.	inscription	_____	_____	
5.	_____	prescribe	_____	
6.	_____	subscribe	_____	
7.	transcription	_____	_____	

Now FILL IN these blanks to complete each word with one of the words above.

1. There is so much in_____ at karate! Girls get treated differently!

2. I don't know what to say. Mrs. Simpson's hair is in_____!

3. Seriously, the lunch lady gives out un_____ portions.

4. I sent in my form to re_____ to my rock collecting magazine.

Keywords

Even though *equal* and *scribe* can stand alone, roots don't usually work by themselves. They need help from prefixes and suffixes. Here are some roots that can't stand alone.

Manually comes from the root "man," which means *hand*.
Corpse comes from the root "corp," which means *body*.
Captain comes from the root "cap," which means *head*.
Capture comes from another root, "cap," which means *to take*.

READ the paragraph. The words in **bold** are your keywords.

On my favorite TV show last night, the cops found a **corpse** inside a **manicure** shop (and it wasn't getting its nails done!)! I guessed right away that the killer was the head of a big **corporation** that **manufactured** robots. I could tell the guy was guilty by his suspicious **manner**. He **demanded** a lawyer, then **managed** to **manipulate** the police into letting him go. The bad guy left the country in a boat. Luckily, the boat **capsized**, and the police **captain commanded** his men to **capture** the criminal.

FILL IN the blanks with the **bold** words in alphabetical order.

1. _____

2. _____

3. _____

4. _____

5. _____

6. _____

7. _____

8. _____

9. _____

10. _____

11. _____

12. _____

✓ **Check It!**

Page 75

Keywords

1. capsized	7. demanded
2. captain	8. managed
3. capture	9. manicure
4. commanded	10. manipulate
5. corporation	11. manner
6. corpse	12. manufactured

Page 76

Stack Up

"Man" Root	"Corp" Root
1. commanded	1. corporation
2. demanded	2. corpse
3. managed	
4. manicure	"Cap" Root
5. manipulate	1. capsized
6. manner	2. captain
7. manufactured	3. capture

Page 77

Word Search

Page 78

Word Blocks

1. Capitol
2. capricious
3. manuscript
4. corpulent
5. manually
6. captor
7. capitalize
8. captive

☑ **Check It!**

Page 79

Morph It!

1. commander, command
2. management, manager, manage
3. manipulation, manipulate
4. incorporate
5. capitalize
6. captor, capture, captive
7. captivate

---

1. manipulative   4. manager
2. commanding   5. captivity
3. captivate   6. capital

Page 80

Pick the One!

1. cap•i•tal•ize   9. man•i•cure
2. ca•pri•cious   10. ma•nip•u•late
3. cap•sized   11. man•ners
4. cap•ti•vate   12. man•u•fac•ture
5. in•cor•po•rat•ed 13. man•u•script
6. cor•po•ral   14. man•u•al•ly
7. cor•pu•lent   15. com•mand•ment
8. man•age•ment   16. de•mand•ing

Stack Up

SORT the keywords by their roots. FILL IN the blanks with the sorted words.

capsized	captain	capture	commanded
corporation	corpse	demanded	managed
manicure	manipulate	manner	manufactured

"Man" Root
Example: manuscript

1. _____

2. _____

3. _____

4. _____

5. _____

6. _____

7. _____

"Corp" Root
Example: corps

1. _____

2. _____

"Cap" Root
Example: captor

1. _____

2. _____

3. _____

Word Search

FILL IN the blanks with forms of the keywords. Then CIRCLE the words in the word grid.
Words go down and across, not diagonally or backwards.

1. John rocked the boat to make it _____ and dump us out.

2. Luke was walking and talking in a strange _____ at the mall today.

3. When I'm sick, I always _____ Mom to make me chicken soup.

4. Hendrick can _____ Lee into doing anything!

5. The team _____ is the one who sets the line-up.

6. My sister always _____ the biggest slice of pie. What a brat!

7. Ew! Your fingernails are a mess. Time to get a _____.

8. Will Lucy ever _____ to get to practice on time?

9. My aunt's company _____ MP3 players. Cool, huh?

10. Aunt June runs a nonprofit _____ that sends medicine to Africa.

C	O	M	M	A	N	D	C	O	R	P	D	E
O	C	A	P	T	A	I	N	X	E	D	Y	W
M	A	N	U	F	A	C	T	U	R	E	S	M
A	P	I	C	V	Q	P	C	A	P	K	T	A
N	S	C	O	R	P	O	R	A	T	I	O	N
N	I	U	R	M	D	E	M	A	N	D	S	A
E	Z	R	P	U	O	O	A	B	M	A	N	G
R	E	E	M	A	N	I	P	U	L	A	T	E

Word Blocks

FILL IN the root "man," "corp," or "cap" in each sentence. Then FILL IN the word blocks with words of the same shape.

HINT: Use the whole word, not just the root.

Fern is so _____ricious! You never know what she'll do next.

Can you open the door _____ually if the electricity goes out?

In the story, a princess was kidnapped. Her _____tor was a smelly pirate.

All the important lawmakers hang out at the _____itol building.

That squirrel is so fat! He's totally _____pulent.

Maybe if you don't _____italize all the letters, it'll be easier to read.

"Let me go, you smelly pirate!" cried the _____tive princess.

Dad's book is just a _____uscript. It hasn't been published yet.

Morph It!

FILL IN the blanks by writing the correct form of the word.

	Noun	Person	Verb	Adjective
1.	commandment	_____	_____	commanding
2.	_____	_____	_____	managerial
3.	_____	manipulator	_____	manipulative
4.	corporation		_____	incorporated
5.	capital	capitalist	_____	capital
6.	captivity	_____	_____	_____
7.	captivation	captivator	_____	captivating

Now FILL IN these blanks with one of the words above.

1. It's very _____ to offer me candy if I'll do what you want.

2. You have to use a _____ voice when you train your dog.

3. Cartoons totally _____ my little brother. You can't tear him away!

4. My sister was promoted to _____ of the restaurant.

5. My mom doesn't believe that wild animals should be kept in _____.

6. Beebee doesn't like to use any _____ letters in her e-mails.

Pick the One!

CIRCLE the correct syllable split for each word.

HINT: Listen to the vowel sounds. You may have to split the root.

Example: demand (de•mand) dem•and

1. capitalize   cap•i•tal•ize   ca•pi•ta•lize

2. capricious   ca•pri•cious   cap•ric•ious

3. capsized   ca•psiz•ed   cap•sized

4. captivate   cap•ti•vate   cap•tiv•ate

5. incorporated   in•corp•or•at•ed   in•cor•po•rat•ed

6. corporal   cor•po•ral   corp•o•ral

7. corpulent   cor•pu•lent   corp•u•lent

8. management   man•ag•ement   man•age•ment

9. manicure   man•ic•ure   man•i•cure

10. manipulate   man•i•pu•late   ma•nip•u•late

11. manners   man•ners   mann•ers

12. manufacture   ma•nu•fact•ure   man•u•fac•ture

13. manuscript   man•u•script   ma•nu•script

14. manually   man•u•al•ly   ma•nu•all•y

15. commandment   comm•and•ment   com•mand•ment

16. demanding   de•mand•ing   dem•and•ing

Keywords

Here are some more roots that can't live on their own:

Dictate comes from the root "dict" (also "dic"), which means *to say*.

Conductor comes from the root "duct" (also "duc"), which means *to lead or take*.

Convert comes from the root "vert" (also "vers"), which means *to turn*.

READ the paragraph. The words in **bold** are your keywords.

> If you look up the word *dictator* in the **dictionary**, you'll see a picture of my gymnastics coach. She **conducts** every training session like she's an army general. No **conversation** allowed! Once she **reduced** Karina to tears because her handstand wasn't perfectly **vertical**. When she **introduced** a new kid and he corrected the way she pronounced his name, she yelled at him for **contradicting** her. After we **educated** our parents about her true nature, our coach **reversed** her behavior for a while. But I **predict** she will soon **revert** to her old ways!

FILL IN the blanks with the **bold** words in alphabetical order.

1. _____ 7. _____

2. _____ 8. _____

3. _____ 9. _____

4. _____ 10. _____

5. _____ 11. _____

6. _____ 12. _____

Check It!

Page 85

Morph It!

1. advertisement
2. contradict
3. conversation
4. convert
5. dedication
6. deduction
7. dictate
8. diversion
9. education
10. introduce
11. production
12. reduction

1. deduction
2. deduce
3. reproduce
4. dictate
5. convert
6. divert

Page 86

Split It!

1. ad•ver•tise
2. ver•ti•cal
3. dic•ta•tor
4. dic•tion•ar•y
5. in•tro•duc•tion
6. de•duc•tion
7. re•pro•duc•tion
8. pro•duc•tion
9. ed•u•ca•tion
10. re•ver•sal
11. con•ver•sion
12. con•ver•sa•tion
13. u•ni•verse
14. di•ver•si•fy
15. in•di•ca•tion
16. ded•i•ca•tion

Stack Up

SORT the keywords by their roots.

conducts	contradicting	conversation	dictator
dictionary	educated	introduced	predict
reduced	revert	reversed	vertical

"Dic/Dict" Root
Example: verdict

1. _____
2. _____
3. _____
4. _____

"Duc/Duct" Root
Example: produce

1. _____
2. _____
3. _____
4. _____

"Vert/Vers" Root
Example: convert

1. _____
2. _____
3. _____
4. _____

Criss Cross

FILL IN the grid by answering the clues with forms of the keywords.

ACROSS

1. A place where you can look up words
4. To lead a class, meeting, or musical group
5. To turn back, go the opposite way
7. To say or guess something before it happens
8. To argue or say the opposite thing

DOWN

1. Someone who tells everyone what to do
2. The act of taking turns talking
3. To make smaller
6. To lead someone toward knowledge

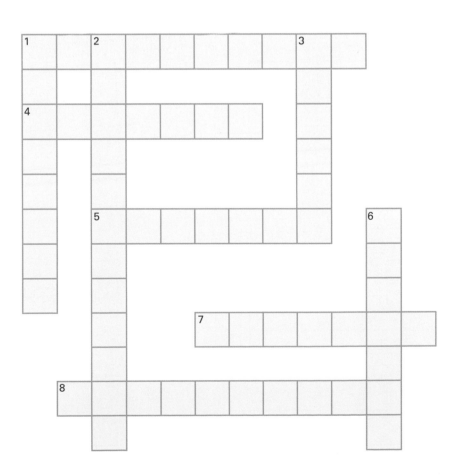

Word Blocks

WRITE the root "dic/dict," "duc/duct," or "vert/vers" in each sentence. Then FILL IN the word blocks with the words of the same shape.

There's a lot of di_____ity in our neighborhood. We're very multiracial.

I'm repro_____ing a famous painting for art class.

Shama answered an ad_____tisement in the paper for a babysitting job.

I love when we drive in the con_____tible with the top down!

The new pool at our YMCA is de_____ated to a kid who died of cancer.

Leonard works on his _____tion in speech class.

Did you hear that the Scoop Shop is intro_____ing a new flavor?

I wonder how many planets are in the uni_____se?

Morph It!

FILL IN the blanks with the correct form of the word.

HINT: All but one of the nouns ends in "ion."

Noun	Verb
1. _____	advertise
2. contradiction	_____
3. _____	converse
4. conversion	_____
5. _____	dedicate
6. _____	deduce
7. dictation	_____
8. _____	divert
9. _____	educate
10. introduction	_____
11. _____	produce
12. _____	reduce

Now FILL IN these blanks with one of the words above.

1. Good detectives are masters of _____.

2. From the mud on your clothes, I _____ you've been outside.

3. Use a photocopier to _____ that newspaper article.

4. My dad has to _____ letters for his assistant to type up.

5. You have to _____ your dollars to pounds when you go to England.

6. Engineers build dams to _____ rivers from their natural course.

Split It!

SPLIT these words into syllables, using dots to mark the breaks.

Example: produce   pro•duce

advertise

vertical

dictator

dictionary

introduction

deduction

reproduction

production

education

reversal

conversion

conversation

universe

diversify

indication

dedication

1. _____

2. _____

3. _____

4. _____

5. _____

6. _____

7. _____

8. _____

9. _____

10. _____

11. _____

12. _____

13. _____

14. _____

15. _____

16. _____

Keywords

Once you know how to spell one word using the root, you should be able to spell most of the words that share the same root. Here are three more roots:

Finish comes from the root "fin," which means *end*.
Avenue comes from the root "ven," which means *come*.
Mission comes from the root "mis" (also "mit"), which means *send*.

READ the paragraph. The words in **bold** are your keywords.

Nothing can **prevent** me from going to the sci-fi **convention**! Last year, I didn't get **permission** to go. So I made a **commitment** to my parents that I would **finish** my homework every night and **submit** to any other chores or commands that they could **invent** for me to do. It **definitely** worked! I now hold in my hands a ticket that says "**admit** one." This will be quite an **adventure**! The grand **finale** will be a special screening of the **final** episode of *Space 2169*, my favorite show. I can't wait!

FILL IN the blanks with the **bold** words in alphabetical order.

1. _____

2. _____

3. _____

4. _____

5. _____

6. _____

7. _____

8. _____

9. _____

10. _____

11. _____

12. _____

Stack Up

SORT the keywords by their roots.

admit	adventure	commitment	convention
definitely	final	finale	finish
invent	permission	prevent	submit

"Fin" Root
Example: finalist

1. _____

2. _____

3. _____

4. _____

"Ven" Root
Example: convenient

1. _____

2. _____

3. _____

4. _____

"Mis/Mit" Root
Example: transmit

1. _____

2. _____

3. _____

4. _____

Word Search

FILL IN the blanks with keywords. Then CIRCLE the words in the word grid. Words go down and across, not diagonally or backwards.

1. Luis has the flu, which will _____ him from going to the picnic.

2. Sheryl likes to read _____ stories, where kids travel and face danger.

3. Someday, I'm going to _____ a car that drives itself.

4. The magician's _____ was to cut a girl in half and make her disappear.

5. You can't go on the trip without your parent's _____.

6. The usher won't _____ you without a ticket.

7. Dad has to go to a _____ of computer programmers. Boring!

8. Serena needs more time so she can _____ her sculpture.

C	O	M	M	P	R	E	M	I	T
C	O	N	V	E	N	T	I	O	N
W	M	I	T	R	L	B	N	P	F
F	V	A	D	M	I	T	V	R	I
I	F	I	N	I	S	H	E	E	N
N	M	I	S	S	V	F	N	V	X
A	F	I	N	S	P	K	T	E	R
L	D	E	F	I	N	E	Q	N	V
E	W	E	C	O	M	M	I	T	E
A	D	V	E	N	T	U	R	E	N

Bonus

There are two words that contain the same root as two keywords. Can you find them?

Morph It!

FILL IN the blanks by writing the correct form of the word.

	Noun	Verb	Adjective	Adverb
1.	invention	_____	_____	inventively
2.	_____	prevent	preventive	_____
3.	_____	permit	_____	permissively
4.	submission	_____	submissive	_____
5.	definition	_____	_____	definitely
6.	commitment	_____		
7.	_____	convene		
8.	admission	_____		

Now FILL IN these blanks with one of the words above.

1. For this show, the price of _____ is ten dollars.

2. Did you _____ your information form online?

3. By coming to practice, you show your _____ to the team.

4. Clara found an _____ way to fix her glasses with a paper clip.

5. We finally sold the house, so our move is now _____.

6. My Dad will _____ all of us when we have a family meeting.

Spotlight on "Nat"

"Nat" means *born*, so a *native* is someone born here. But there's more to "nat" than meets the eye. Say these two words out loud: *natural* and *nature*. The first syllables sound different, right? Let's take a closer look, using these keywords:

SORT these words, and SPLIT them into syllables, using dots to mark the breaks.

nation	national	native	natural	nature
prenatal	supernatural	multinational	innate	

Long "A" Sound
Example: ba•by

1. _____

2. _____

3. _____

4. _____

5. _____

Short "A" Sound
Example: bab•ble

1. _____

2. _____

3. _____

4. _____

Author! Author!

It's your turn to do the writing. Use at least six of these words to write a story, a poem, or a list of crazy sentences. Have fun!

equalize	scribble	subscribe	manicure	demand	corpse
corpulent	captive	dictator	introduce	reduce	advertise

Stack Up

SORT the words by their roots.

commandment   controversy   demanding   diversion

indescribable   invert   manipulate   mission

permissive   prescribe   transcription   transmit

"Script/Scrib" Root (To Write)
Example: scribble

1. _____

2. _____

3. _____

"Man" Root (Hand)
Example: scribble

1. _____

2. _____

3. _____

"Vert" Root (To Turn)
Example: convert

1. _____

2. _____

3. _____

"Mit" Root (To Send)
Example: admission

1. _____

2. _____

3. _____

Criss Cross

FILL IN the grid by answering the clues.

HINT: Don't forget to use a dictionary if you need help!

ACROSS

2. You just can't even say how it was!

4. An order you must obey

6. An argument over an opinion

7. To turn something upside-down

8. A job or task you are sent to do

DOWN

1. Really easygoing, allowing a lot

3. Constantly asking for things

5. It turns you away from your course

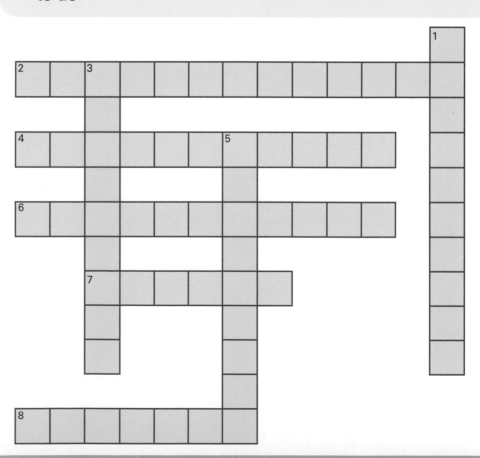

Pick the One!

CIRCLE the correct answer to each clue.

Example: Someone who teaches is an (educator) *edictator*

1. When you say something beforehand   prescription   prediction

2. To turn back to the way you were   revert   reduce

3. The last act of a show is the   finale   capital

4. When day and night are the same length   corpinox   equinox

5. Something you write by hand   interscript   manuscript

6. To take someone away   capture   captive

7. Someone who tells everybody what to do   ductator   dictator

8. To make a copy   produce   reproduce

9. If you lead the band, you are the   conductor   conducter

10. Stop something from happening   prevent   prescribe

11. Turned straight up and down   corporal   vertical

12. Before birth   prenatural   prenatal

13. To send something across space   transmit   transduce

14. With no ending   incapable   infinite

15. Having equal sides   multilateral   equilateral

16. Very fat   capulent   corpulent

17. To take things into your own hands   manage   convene

Morph It!

FILL IN the blanks by writing the correct form of the word.

Noun	Verb	Adjective	Adverb
1. _____	capitalize	_____	capitally
2. _____	_____	captivating	_____
3. _____	_____	commanding	_____
4. _____	_____	_____	conversationally
5. _____	define	_____	_____
6. _____	_____	educational	_____
7. _____	equalize	equal	_____
8. equation	equate	_____	equitably
9. _____	invent	inventive	_____
10. _____	_____	_____	managerially

Keywords

Some words sound the same but are spelled differently. These words are called HOMOPHONES. Sometimes, two words sound the same because they have similar (but not identical) prefixes or suffixes.

READ the paragraph. The words in **bold** are your keywords.

In the movie *Castle Crash*, the hero is all set to marry a princess, **except** her family won't **accept** him. Have you **seen** it? The best **scene** is when he has to hide in a basement, standing up to his **waist** in disgusting sewer **waste** and sludge. But all that muck doesn't **lessen** our hero's courage! He plans to teach the royal family a **lesson**. He sneaks in while **they're** asleep in **their** rooms. But the family has a **guest** (an old lady), and she's **guessed** his plan. I won't tell you how it ends. But it's so exciting!

FILL IN the blanks with the **bold** words in alphabetical order.

1. _____
2. _____
3. _____
4. _____
5. _____
6. _____
7. _____
8. _____
9. _____
10. _____
11. _____
12. _____

✓ Check It!

Page 101

Spell Check

1. chews	9. too
2. banned	10. world
3. overseas	11. guest
4. peak	12. sense
5. colonel	13. praise
6. principal	14. lessen
7. weight	15. They're
8. waste	16. guilt

Page 102

Spotlight on Homographs

1. i	9. l
2. k	10. n
3. o	11. b
4. a	12. e
5. f	13. p
6. c	14. d
7. m	15. g
8. j	16. h

Blank Out!

FILL IN the blanks with the correct keyword to finish the sentence.

1. My little sister always cries and makes a _____ when she doesn't get her way.

2. Lorna was mean to every _____ at her party.

3. I like everything about Raoul _____ his bad breath.

4. Mom gave me an aspirin to _____ the pain after I banged my head.

5. That outfit would look better with a belt around your _____.

6. My parents are so weird. Today, _____ wearing matching jackets!

7. My pal Duncan says talking to girls is a _____ of time.

8. The twins are hungry. Are _____ bottles ready?

9. I can't find my sunglasses. Have you _____ them?

12. Fiona has to go to her piano _____ right after lunch.

Criss Cross

FILL IN the grid by answering the clues with keywords.

ACROSS

1. Figured out, or tried to

4. To make less

6. A word you use to leave something out

7. A contraction

DOWN

1. Someone who goes to a party

2. A section of a show or a play

3. About halfway between your neck and your knees

5. Welcome or receive

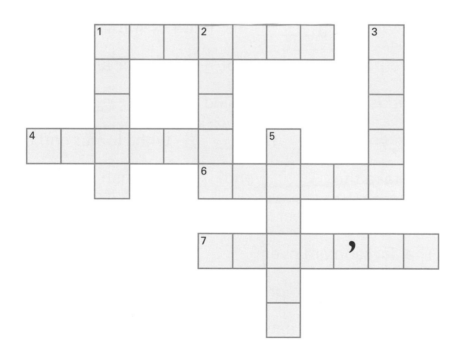

Blank Out!

FILL IN the blanks with the correct word to finish the sentence.

Example: threw/through: Arnold threw *the ball* through *the hoop.*

billed/build: 1. The carpenter _____ my parents $100 to _____ the shelves.

aloud/allowed: 2. No one's _____ to read _____ at the library.

Capitol/capital: 3. The _____ building is spelled with a _____ letter "c."

close/clothes: 4. I'm very _____ to filling my closet with new _____.

flew/flu: 5. When Mom got the _____, we _____ home from Florida early.

medal/metal: 6. My swimming _____ is made of shiny gold _____.

pears/pairs: 7. We're painting _____ of _____ for art class.

too/to: 8. Ingrid is going _____ sled with us _____!

seen/scene: 9. Have you _____ the _____ with Homer and the bear?

we'll/wheel: 10. You take the _____ and _____ push the car.

overdue/overdo: 11. I know your project is _____, but don't _____ it!

there/their: 12. The Jackson are over _____, washing_____car.

your/you're: 13. _____ going to drop _____ ice cream!

colonel/kernel: 14. _____ Chavez eats his popcorn one _____ at a time.

banned/band: 15. Our _____ was _____ from the fair because we're too loud.

weight/wait: 16. _____ for help before trying to lift that much _____.

sense/cents: 17. If Jolene had any _____, she'd have saved more than fifty

_____ by now.

Spell Check

READ each sentence. CIRCLE the homophone that's wrong. Then WRITE the RIGHT homophone in the blank.

Example: We burn would in our fireplace. <u>wood</u>

1. Toby choose gum all the time! _____

2. Too bad they band chewing gum at school. _____

3. Have you ever traveled oversees? _____

4. Uncle Jim climbed Mount Kisco's highest peek. _____

5. Simka's mom is a kernel in the army. _____

6. Who would ever want to be a school principle? _____

7. I bet you can't lift that heavy wait! _____

8. Don't waist so much paper! Use both sides. _____

9. That pot is two hot to touch! Use an oven mitt. _____

10. I want to travel all over the whirled. _____

11. Be my guessed! _____

12. Wearing a bike helmet is common cents. _____

13. People always prays my mom's apple pie. _____

14. If you take an aspirin, it will lesson the pain. _____

15. The Rubins called. There not coming over tonight. _____

16. I'm feeling some gilt about not helping set the table. _____

Spotlight on Homographs

Some words are spelled the same but sound different (the opposite of homophones!). These are called HOMOGRAPHS. Sometimes, changing the vowel sound gives a word a different meaning. You already know how to spell these words, so don't be confused by the way they sound!

DRAW a line to connect each word on the left with the correct meaning on the right.

Multiple Meaning Word
Example: read (rhymes with red)

Definition
past tense of to read

1. dove (rhymes with love) ____
2. dove (rhymes with stove) ____
3. bow (rhymes with now) ____
4. bow (rhymes with snow) ____
5. wind (rhymes with pinned) ____
6. wind (rhymes with kind) ____
7. lead (rhymes with red) ____
8. lead (rhymes with feed) ____
9. tear (rhymes with stare) ____
10. tear (rhymes with steer) ____
11. bass (rhymes with space) ____
12. bass (rhymes with pass) ____
13. sow (rhymes with now) ____
14. sow (rhymes with snow) ____
15. live (rhymes with give) ____
16. live (rhymes with drive) ____

a. hair ribbon
b. low musical sound or guitar
c. to twist and turn
d. to plant seeds
e. a kind of fish
f. gusty breeze
g. to breathe, exist
h. not dead
i. a kind of bird
j. to go in front, take charge
k. past tense of *to dive*
l. to rip
m. kind of metal or past tense verb *to lead*
n. drop that comes from your eyes
o. to bend over
p. mama pig

Keywords

The harder the word, the harder the homophone. Once you get a handle on these words, you'll be a super speller!

READ the paragraph. The words in **bold** are your keywords.

Vincent won't **loan** me ten bucks to go to the carnival at the **naval** air base, even though he's the **heir** to some giant fortune. I guess cheapness is in his **genes**, because his dad's that way too. And now I'm **mourning** the fact that I have to get new **jeans** because I ripped mine this **morning** trying to climb the carnival fence. Well, that effort was totally in **vain**, plus I got a cut just above my **navel**, which is bleeding like crazy. It must've hit a **vein**. Mom says even though I'm the **lone** kid in the house, I make enough trouble for ten. Whatever!

FILL IN the blanks with the **bold** words in alphabetical order.

1. _____   7. _____

2. _____   8. _____

3. _____   9. _____

4. _____   10. _____

5. _____   11. _____

6. _____   12. _____

✓ **Check It!**

Page 103

Keywords

1. air
2. genes
3. heir
4. jeans
5. loan
6. lone
7. morning
8. mourning
9. naval
10. navel
11. vain
12. vein

Page 104

Blank Out!

1. lone
2. jeans
3. heir
4. navel
5. vein
6. mourning
7. naval
8. genes
9. vain
10. loan

Page 105

Word Blocks

1. bolder
2. naval
3. affect
4. prey
5. bread
6. passed

Page 106

Blank Out!

1. udder, utter
2. sealing, ceiling
3. foreword, forward
4. pray, prey
5. stationary, stationery
6. lightning, lightening
7. past, passed
8. vain, vein

✓ # Check It!

Page 107

Spell Check

1. mantel	9. core
2. effect	10. navel
3. edition	11. genes
4. except	12. lightening
5. weighs	13. affect
6. prey	14. principles
7. bred	15. profit
8. boulder	16. ceiling

Page 108

Spotlight

1. CONduct, conDUCT
2. CONflict, conFLICT
3. CONtent, conTENT
4. CONtest, conTEST
5. reCORD, REcord
6. obJECT, OBject
7. proTEST, PROtest
8. reFUSE, REFuse

1. CONtest, conTEST
2. conDUCT, CONduct
3. CONtent, conTENT
4. obJECT, OBject

Blank Out!

FILL IN the blanks with the correct keyword to finish the sentence.

1. No one else could go to the party, so I was the
   _____ guest.

2. Cassie wears her favorite _____ twice a week.

3. The _____ to the king will someday get the crown.

4. My sister's _____ is an "outtie," but mine's an "innie."

5. Honoria is so pale, you can see every _____ in her neck.

6. Mrs. Stein is still in _____ for Elvis, even though he died
   like a million years ago!

7. Dad took us to see the ships at the _____ museum.

8. Lila thinks she'll live to be a
   hundred, because she's got good _____.

9. Luke dove to the ground in a _____ attempt to catch the
   ball. He failed.

10. Hey, would you _____ me five bucks? I'm good for it!

Word Blocks

FILL IN the word blocks with words of the same shape to finish the homophone pair.

Example:

b i l l e d

b u i l d

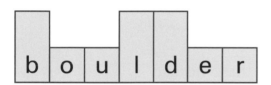

b o u l d e r

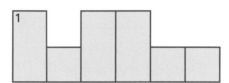

1

n a v e l

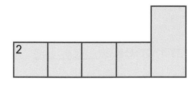

2

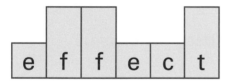

e f f e c t

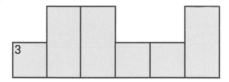

3

p r a y

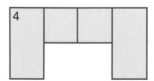

4

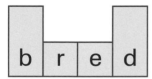

b r e d

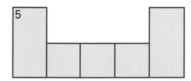

5

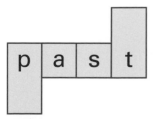

p a s t

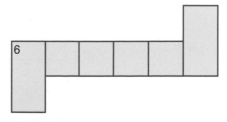

6

Harder Homophones

Blank Out!

FILL IN the blanks with the right homophones.

utter
udder

1. Anna touched the cow's

   _____ with a look of _____ disgust.

ceiling
sealing

2. The handyman is _____ all the cracks in

   our _____.

foreword
forward

3. In the book's _____, the author looks

   _____ to the future.

prey
pray

4. Let's _____ that that big hawk doesn't think of us

   as _____.

stationary
stationery

5. While the train is _____, I'll write a letter on my

   new _____.

lightening
lightning

6. Bolts of _____ were _____ the sky in

   flashes.

past
passed

7. My fight with Judi is in the _____. A lot of time

   has _____ since then.

vein
vain

8. My mom is very _____, and she hates that

   _____ sticking out of her forehead.

Spell Check

READ each sentence. CIRCLE the homophone that's wrong. Then WRITE the RIGHT homophone in the blank.

1. Mom loves that ugly clock on the fireplace mantle. _____

2. The cold weather doesn't have any affect on me. _____

3. I can't wait to get the next addition of *Comics Monthly*! _____

4. Katrina is a nice girl, accept she talks a lot. _____

5. I bet my brain ways 300 pounds! _____

6. Kitty Fluff-Fluff is stalking her pray. _____

7. Pugs were bread to be lap dogs. Aren't they cute? _____

8. Watch out! That big bolder is about to fall off the cliff! _____

9. Don't leave that apple corps on the table! _____

10. Gina drew a face on her belly and her naval was the nose. _____

11. I inherited my dad's jeans, which gave me blue eyes. _____

12. Luis is lightning up his room with yellow paint. _____

13. If we lose this game, it will effect our standings. _____

14. Kirby is trying to teach me the basic principals of chess. _____

15. We made a big prophet from our band candy sale. _____

16. Eek! There's a giant spider on the sealing! _____

Spotlight on Stressing Out with Homographs

You know how to STRESS a syllable, right? It means you say it louder. Some homographs sound different because of the syllable that gets stressed, but these words are still spelled same way. For example, DESert vs. deSERT.

READ the words twice, putting the stress first on one syllable, then the other.

		Stress First Syllable	**Stress Second Syllable**
1.	conduct	behavior	to lead
2.	conflict	a war or battle	to disagree or clash
3.	content	information or insides	happy
4.	contest	a game or match	to disagree or fight against
5.	record	a saved sound or event	to save a sound or event
6.	object	a thing	be against something
7.	protest	a public complaint	to voice a complaint
8.	refuse	garbage	to say no

Most of the time, stressing the first syllable means a noun, and stressing the second syllable means a verb. CIRCLE the stressed syllable for each **bold** word.

1. Khaled won the **contest**, but Ricky will **contest** the results.

2. You **conduct** the band well, but your personal **conduct** is very bad.

3. That game site has so much **content**! It'll keep me **content** for a while.

4. You can hardly **object** to such a harmless **object**.

Keywords

Time to level up! If you want to be a true spelling master, you need to learn some tough words.

READ the paragraph. The words in **bold** are your keywords.

I have zero **experience** with fame, but I know that **publicity** is very important. I mean, actors love to be recognized by **enthusiastic** fans. And some people do **mischievous** things just to get their names in the paper. But others work hard to keep everyone **ignorant** of their **identity**. Like, in order to **detect** spies or gather **intelligence**, secret agents need to **preserve** their "cover." They have to **behave** as normally as possible, so they don't attract **suspicion**. As for me, I'm going into **politics**, so I need all the publicity I can get!

FILL IN the blanks with the **bold** words in alphabetical order.

1. _____
2. _____
3. _____
4. _____
5. _____
6. _____

7. _____
8. _____
9. _____
10. _____
11. _____
12. _____

✓ Check It!

Page 109

Keywords

1. behave	7. intelligence
2. detect	8. mischievous
3. enthusiastic	9. politics
4. experience	10. preserve
5. identity	11. publicity
6. ignorant	12. suspicion

Page 110
Morph It!

1. behavior, behavioral
2. detectably
3. enthusiasm, enthusiastic
4. experience
5. identity, identifiably
6. ignorance, ignorant
7. intelligence, intelligently
8. mischievous, mischievously
9. politics, political
10. preservation
11. publicity, publicly
12. suspicious, suspiciously

Page 111
Criss Cross

Across	Down
1. enthusiasm	1. experience
4. intelligent	2. identity
5. behavior	3. mischievous
7. publicize	4 ignorance

Page 112
Spell Check

1. suspicion	9. preservation
2. identify	10. ignorance
3. political	11. intelligently
4. behavioral	12. undetectable
5. publicly	13. inexperienced
6. detective	14. politicize
7. enthusiastically	15. unidentifiable
8. mischief	16. misbehaved

Morph It!

FILL IN the blanks by writing the correct form of the word.

	Noun	Adjective	Adverb
1.	_____	_____	behaviorally
2.	detective	detectable	_____
3.	_____	_____	enthusiastically
4.	_____	experienced	
5.	_____	identifiable	_____
6.	_____	_____	ignorantly
7.	_____	intelligent	_____
8.	mischief	_____	_____
9.	_____	_____	politically
10.	_____	preservative	
11.	_____	public	_____
12.	suspicion	_____	_____

Criss Cross

FILL IN the grid by answering the clues with versions of keywords.

ACROSS

1. Excitement, energy, delight

4. Smart

5. The way you act (good or bad)

7. To make public

DOWN

1. If you've done it before, you've got ___.

2. Your name and other information about you

3. Wicked, annoying, or bad

4. State of being uninformed

Spell Check

READ each sentence. CIRCLE the word that's wrong. Then FILL IN the blanks with the correct words. Spell them right!

1. I have a strong suspectment that I'm getting an MP3 player. _____

2. Investigators can identize a corpse by its teeth. _____

3. This country has two main politicious parties. _____

4. My little brother has behavement problems. _____

5. The star publically denied the rumor about losing his dog. _____

6. Sherlock Holmes is my favorite detector. He's a genius! _____

7. My dog Pepper always greets me enthusiastially. _____

8. October 30th is mischievement night in our town. _____

9. The preservement of old movies is so important. _____

10. Will you live your whole life in ignorification of inequality? _____

11. My Dad always explains things very intelligencely. _____

12. There was a nearly undetectifiable smell of wet dog. _____

13. I'm too inexperiencious to ski down a steep mountain. _____

14. The newspapers tried to politify the mayor's wedding. _____

15. With his new beard and glasses, Mr. Hinks is unidentical. _____

16. I'm dead tired. The girl I baby-sit misbehaviored all day! _____

Spotlight on Compound Words

As you already know, a compound word is a word made by sticking two words together. As the words get harder to spell, so do the compounds. Let's pound a few together and see!

MATCH a word on the left with one on the right to make a compound. DRAW a line to connect the two words. FILL IN the blanks with the compound words you matched.

SPLIT the words into syllables, using dots to mark the breaks.

Example: cow   boy   <u>cow•boy</u>

1.	button	friend	_____
2.	care	water	_____
3.	eye	room	_____
4.	body	way	_____
5.	girl	mint	_____
6.	ever	kind	_____
7.	finger	guard	_____
8.	fresh	kerchief	_____
9.	hand	green	_____
10.	high	spoon	_____
11.	jelly	apple	_____
12.	human	hole	_____
13.	pepper	taker	_____
14.	pine	bean	_____
15.	show	glasses	_____
16.	table	nail	_____

Author! Author!

It's your turn to do the writing. Use at least six of the words to write a story, a poem, or a list of crazy sentences. Have fun!

banned	bass	contest	guilty
lightning	medal	mischief	navel
overdue	praise	suspicious	verse

_____

_____

_____

_____

_____

_____

_____

_____

_____

_____

_____

_____

_____

_____

_____

_____

Stack Up

SORT the words into the categories.

accept	adventure	behavioral	bodyguard
colonel	energetic	except	handkerchief
inventor	kernel	permissive	prevention

"Ven" Root
Example: convene

1. _____

2. _____

3. _____

Adjectives
Example: suspicious

1. _____

2. _____

3. _____

Homophones
Example: past/passed

1. _____ / _____

2. _____ / _____

Compound Words
Example: jellybean

1. _____

2. _____

Blank Out!

FILL IN the blanks with the correct roots. You can use the roots more than once.

fin	mit	ven	dic/dict	duc/duct
man	corp	cap	equi/equa	vert/vers

1. A dead body   ___ ___ ___ ___se

2. To change into something else   con___ ___ ___ ___

3. Where the government hangs out   ___ ___ ___itol

4. To give in   sub___ ___ ___

5. Make a copy   repro___ ___ ___e

6. To take things into your own hands   ___ ___ ___age

7. Different, varied, multicultural   di___ ___ ___ ___e

8. To say or guess something beforehand   pre___ ___ ___ ___

9. Very exciting, possibly dangerous   ad___ ___ ___turous

10. To end something   ___ ___ ___ish

11. When day and night are the same length   ___ ___ ___ ___nox

12. Someone who has been taken   ___ ___ ___tive

13. To control someone   ___ ___ ___ipulate

14. Easy, not a hassle at all   con___ ___ ___ient

15. To lead, like a band   con___ ___ ___ ___

16. To let someone in, or to confess   ad___ ___ ___

17. With no ending   in___ ___ ___ite

18. When everyone is treated the same   ___ ___ ___ ___lity

Word Blocks

FILL IN the word blocks with words of the same shape to finish the homophone pair.

Example:

 p a s t

p a s s e d

 m a n t l e

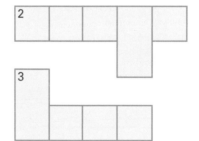 1

 c o r e

 2

3

 a i r

 m o r n i n g

 4

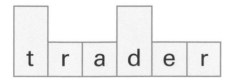 t r a d e r

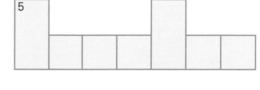 5

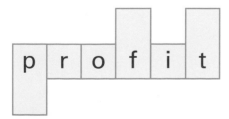 p r o f i t

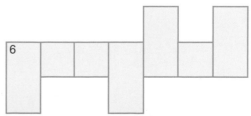 6

Morph It!

FILL IN the blanks by writing the correct form of the word.

	Noun	Verb	Adjective	Adverb
1.				disagreeably
2.	apology			
3.			civil	
4.		compete		
5.		confuse	confusing	
6.		contradict		
7.		decide		
8.		define		
9.		describe		descriptively
10.	energy			

accept	complaining	enclosed	frosty
accompaniment	composition	enraged	genes
admit	conducts	enriching	guessed
adventure	confused	enthusiastic	guest
adventurous	constantly	entitled	heir
air	contradicting	entrapped	horrified
ambition	convention	equally	hospitalized
antibiotics	conversation	equates	humorous
antiperspirant	corporation	equations	identify
antisocial	corpse	equator	identity
antiwar	crazy	equivalent	ignorant
anxiously	creative	except	immature
apologized	criticized	excitable	impatient
arrangement	decisive	excitement	impolite
behave	definitely	experience	improvement
brainy	demanded	famous	inconvenient
bridal	describes	final	indirect
capsized	detect	finale	inexcusable
captain	dictator	finish	inexpensive
capture	dictionary	flawlessly	inscription
challenger	disapprove	forecast	instruction
commanded	disobey	forefinger	instructor
commitment	disrespectful	foreground	intelligence
communicate	educated	forehead	interact
competition	employment	foremost	interactive
competitive	empowered	formal	Internet

Spelling Words Index

4th-Grade Vocabulary Success

Keywords

a•muse—uh-MYOOZ *verb* 1. to charm or entertain 2. to make smile or laugh
Synonyms: charm, entertain, delight. Antonyms: bore, tire.

bud•dy—BUH-dee *noun* friend
Synonyms: pal, friend, chum. Antonyms: enemy, foe.

dis•con•tin•ue—DIS-kuhn-TIHN-yoo *verb* to stop doing something
Synonyms: stop, end, terminate. Antonyms: continue, proceed, persist.

en•a•ble—ehn-AY-buhl *verb* to make possible
Synonyms: allow, permit, let. Antonyms: prevent, stop, prohibit.

im•mense—ih-MEHNS *adjective* very large
Synonyms: huge, vast, massive. Antonyms: tiny, minute, small.

in•tel•li•gent—ihn-TEHL-uh-juhnt *adjective* smart
Synonyms: smart, bright, clever. Antonyms: stupid, ignorant, dense.

plunge—pluhnj *verb* 1. to move abruptly forward or downward 2. to thrust
into something
Synonyms: dive, plummet. Antonyms: leap, climb.

po•lite—puh-LIT *adjective* showing good manners
Synonyms: respectful, courteous. Antonyms: rude, impolite, offensive.

prob•a•bly—PRAHB-uh-blee *adverb* very likely
Synonyms: likely, doubtless. Antonyms: unlikely, doubtfully.

re•lax—rih-LAKS *verb* 1. to loosen up 2. to make less strict
Synonyms: unwind, loosen up, calm down. Antonyms: tense up, stiffen, strain.

✓ Check It!

Page 124
Read & Replace

1. immense
2. buddy
3. probably
4. polite
5. discontinue
6. enable
7. plunge
8. relax
9. amuse
10. intelligent

Page 125
Blank Out!

1. buddy
2. relax
3. probably
4. amuse
5. discontinue
6. intelligent
7. polite
8. enable
9. immense
10. plunge

Page 126
Tic-Tac-Toe

1. pal, friend, ally
2. bore, depress, annoy
3. stop, halt, cease
4. mannerly, courteous, considerate

Page 127
Criss Cross

ACROSS	DOWN
1. polite	1. plunge
2. buddy	3. discontinue
5. immense	4. amuse
6. enable	
7. intelligent	
8. relax	

Synonyms & Antonyms

Check It!

Page 128

Petal Power

1. buddy
2. enable
3. immense
4. intelligent
5. probably

Page 129

Night & Day

1. i 6. e
2. j 7. h
3. a 8. d
4. c 9. g
5. f 10. b

Page 130

Blank Out!

1. polite
2. intelligent
3. discontinue
4. probably
5. amuse
6. buddy
7. enable
8. plunge
9. relax
10. immense

Read & Replace

READ the paragraph. The **bold** words are SYNONYMS to the keywords. Synonyms are words that have the same meanings, like *small* and *little*. Then FILL IN the blanks in the second paragraph with keywords.

amuse	buddy	enable	immense	discontinue
intelligent	plunge	polite	probably	relax

Dear Mom and Dad,

Thanks for the 1 _____ care package you sent.
huge

My 2 _____ Rick 3 _____ ate half
pal **quite likely**

the cookies by himself. I was 4 _____ but made
courteous

him 5 _____ pigging out! The money you included
stop

will 6 _____ me to buy some snacks at the
allow

Trading Post. Right now, though, it's so hot I need to take

a 7 _____ in the cool water. Then I will
dive

8 _____ and let my friends 9 _____
unwind **entertain**

me with their stupid jokes. (Don't get me wrong—my friends

are very 10 _____. It's just their jokes that aren't!)
smart

Can't wait to see you on Visiting Day!

Max

124

Blank Out!

FILL IN the blanks with keywords. Each sentence contains an ANTONYM of a keyword in **bold**. Antonyms are words that have opposite meanings, like *fast* and *slow*.

amuse	buddy	enable	immense	discontinue
intelligent	plunge	polite	probably	relax

1. At first she was my **enemy**, but now she's my _____.

2. If studying made you **tense**, you can _____ by shooting some hoops.

3. It seemed **unlikely** that she would win, but she will _____ be the class

   president.

4. Though the first act might **bore** you, the second one will definitely

   _____ you.

5. Hit "OK" to **keep going** or "Cancel" to _____.

6. Many people think birds are **stupid**, but they are actually very _____.

7. Even though my brother is **rude** to me, I try to be _____ to him.

8. Playing basketball might **prevent** you from getting better, but staying home will

   _____ you to get well.

9. We walked through a **little** park

   and then got to an

   _____ field.

10. The rollercoaster **climbed** to

    the top before it began to

    _____ downward.

Tic-Tac-Toe

PLAY Tic-tac-toe with synonyms and antonyms. CIRCLE any word that is a synonym to the blue word. PUT an X through any antonyms. When you find three synonyms or antonyms in a row, you are a winner! The line can go up and down, across, or diagonally.

HINT: If you find a word you don't know, check a dictionary or thesaurus.

Example:

fast

slow	rapid	lazy
crawling	racing	quick
speedy	swift	sluggish

1. buddy

opponent	rival	partner
chum	enemy	foe
pal	friend	ally

2. amuse

entertain	bore	make laugh
please	depress	annoy
aggravate	annoy	charm

3. discontinue

stop	start	abort
halt	continue	maintain
cease	quit	continue

4. polite

mannerly	courteous	considerate
respectful	rude	impolite
crude	refined	nasty

Criss Cross

FILL IN the grid by answering the clues with keywords. The clues are all synonyms of the keywords.

ACROSS

1. Say thank you to be _____.
2. To be safe, stick with your ____ on the field trip.
5. The size of an elephant
6. Help something happen
7. Smart
8. Let loose

DOWN

1. When you don't hesitate to get in the pool
3. Cease
4. Delight

Petal Power

The petals around the flowers are ANTONYMS to the word in the center. Antonyms are words that have opposite meanings, like *tiny* and *huge*. READ the words around each flower. Then WRITE the keyword that's their antonym in the center.

buddy   enable   immense   intelligent   probably

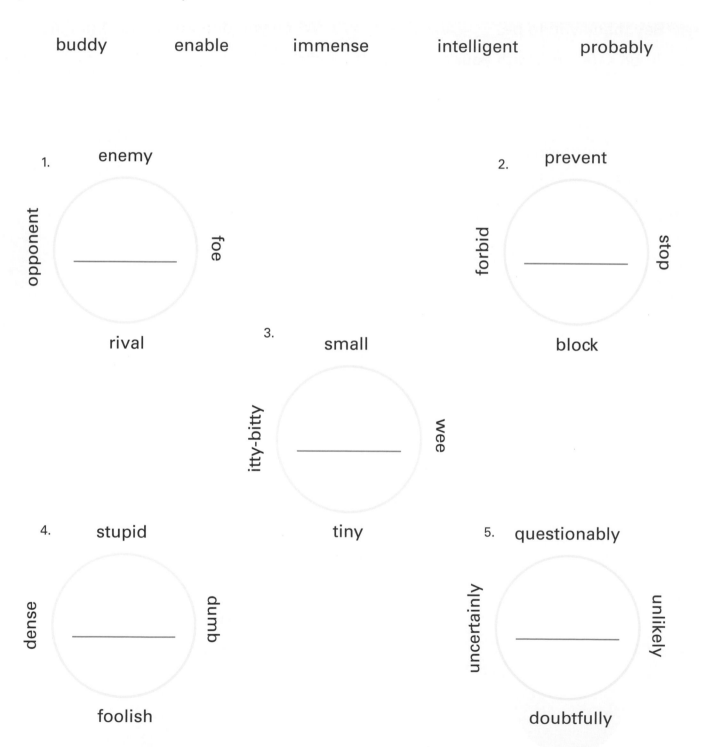

1. enemy

opponent   _____   foe

rival

2. prevent

forbid   _____   stop

block

3. small

itty-bitty   _____   wee

tiny

4. stupid

dense   _____   dumb

foolish

5. questionably

uncertainly   _____   unlikely

doubtfully

Night & Day

MATCH each word in the moon column to its antonym in the sun column.

1. plunge

2. probably

3. enable

4. polite

5. intelligent

6. immense

7. relax

8. discontinue

9. amuse

10. buddy

a. prevent

b. enemy

c. rude

d. keep going

e. small

f. stupid

g. bore

h. tense up

i. climb

j. unlikely

Blank Out!

FILL in the blanks with keywords.

1. Saying "please" and "thank you" is being _____.

2. Someone who gets straight A's is _____.

3. When you no longer want a magazine subscription, you _____ it.

4. I brought my umbrella because the weather report said that it would

   _____ rain.

5. Jokes and riddles _____ us.

6. I like to hang out with my _____.

7. When you help someone get something done, you _____ them.

8. If it's hot tomorrow, let's _____ into a cool pool.

9. After raking leaves for hours, I like to _____.

10. Something humongous is _____.

 **Check It!**

Cut out the Check It! section on page 123, and see if you got the answers right.

Keywords

a•loud—uh-LOWD *adverb* 1. using the voice 2. not silently

al•lowed—uh-LOWD *verb (past tense)* permitted

creak—kreek *verb* to make a squeaking sound

creek—kreek *noun* a small stream

hour—owr *noun* 1. a unit of time equaling 60 minutes 2. the time of day

our—owr *pronoun* belonging to us

prin•ci•pal—PRIHN-suh-puhl *noun* 1. the head of a school 2. the main leader of an activity or group

prin•ci•ple—PRIHN-suh-puhl *noun* a belief or value that helps guide behavior

sighs—siz *verb* breathes out audibly *noun* the sounds of sighing

size—siz *noun* 1. how big something is 2. the physical dimensions of an object

---

✓ Check It!

Page 132

Blank Out!

1. principal
2. our
3. creek
4. hour
5. aloud
6. allowed
7. size
8. creak
9. principle
10. sighs

Page 133

Homophone Hopscotch

1. hour
2. principal
3. sighs
4. our
5. allowed
6. creak
7. principle
8. size
9. aloud
10. creak

Page 134

It's Puzzling!

1. aloud, D. allowed
2. creak, B. creek
3. principal, E. principle
4. size, A. sighs
5. our, C. hour

Page 135

Criss Cross

ACROSS	DOWN
2. our	1. principal
3. size	3. sighs
5. hour	4. creak
7. allowed	6. creek

 **Check It!**

Page 136

Blank Out!

1. hour
2. size
3. allowed
4. creak
5. sighs
6. principle
7. aloud
8. our
9. principal
10. creek

Page 137

Double Trouble

1. principal
2. allowed
3. sighs
4. hour
5. principle
6. our
7. aloud
8. creak
9. size
10. creek

Page 138

Blank Out!

1. size
2. principle
3. our
4. allowed
5. aloud
6. sighs
7. creek
8. principal
9. creak
10. hour

Blank Out!

HOMOPHONES are words that sound the same but have different meanings. *Too*, *two*, and *to* are homophones. READ the story. Then FILL IN the blanks with keywords.

aloud	allowed	creak	creek	hour
our	principal	principle	sighs	size

We had an assembly at school today. The 1_____

told us that a special activity was going to take place that

afternoon. As part of a nature program, 2_____

entire grade was going to walk to a nearby 3_____.

We would spend an 4_____ studying the land,

water, and wildlife. She said that no talking 5_____

would be 6_____. I knew that would be hard for my

buddy, Benny.

The creek was small, but I could not believe the 7_____

of the frogs and minnows. Right off, Benny fell in! His wet shoes

started to 8_____. That scared all the frogs away!

Then he began making *ribbit!* noises, hopping like a frog and

chasing after them. Thanks to Benny, we all got a lesson on the

9_____ of not disturbing nature. And the teacher

learned not to go with Benny on any more nature walks! All too

soon, the hour was up. There were many 10_____

from the teacher as we headed back inside.

Homophone Hopscotch

LOOK AT the definitions. FIND the matching keyword, and put it in the box with the same number.

aloud	allowed	creak	creek	hour
our	principal	principle	sighs	size

1. 60 minutes

2. head of school

3. lets out a loud breath

4. belonging to us

5. permitted

6. small stream

7. strong belief

8. how big something is

9. not silently

10. squeaking sound

10. _____

8. _____   9. _____

7. _____

5. _____   6. _____

4. _____

2. _____   3. _____

1. _____

Bonus

SHADE in the boxes with colored pencils. Use the same color for each pair of homophones.

It's Puzzling!

FILL IN a keyword to solve each clue. MATCH each puzzle piece to its homophone partner.

how you say
something when
you want to
be heard

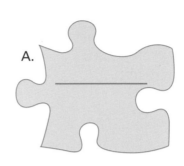

long deep
breaths of relief

the sound an
old door makes

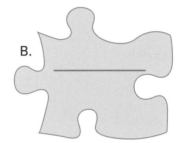

small stream

the head of
your school

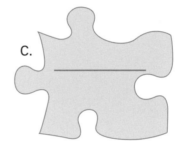

from 2:00 to
3:00

how big
something is

not forbidden

belonging to
you and me

what makes
you do the right
thing

Criss Cross

FILL IN the grid by answering the clues with keywords.

ACROSS

2. We share a book, so it's ___ book.

3. Physical dimensions

5. Unit of time

7. You're not ___ to go there.

DOWN

1. Vice principal's boss

3. Sounds of relief or boredom

4. Old floorboards sometimes do this

6. A place where you might catch small fish

Blank Out!

FILL in the blanks with keywords.

aloud	allowed	creak	creek	hour
our	principal	principle	sighs	size

1. Henry had to practice piano for an _____ before he could play

   basketball.

2. When she reeled it in, Lisa couldn't believe the _____ of the fish.

3. Nate was _____ to stay up later than his little brother.

4. Keely tiptoed, trying not to let the floor _____.

5. We let out _____ of relief when we heard there was no homework.

6. Stella went back to return the change as a matter of _____.

7. Sammy kept his thoughts to himself rather than saying them _____.

8. After the other team's third out, it will be _____ turn at bat.

9. Our school's _____ told us tomorrow is

   Silly Hat Day.

10. There has been so much rain that the

    _____ may overflow.

Double Trouble

CIRCLE the keyword that completes each sentence.

1. Make sure to see the principle / principal for a late pass.

2. No one is allowed / aloud to come into my room without permission.

3. My mother always size / sighs if we leave our shoes in the middle of the floor.

4. The brownies took an hour / our to bake and only ten minutes to eat!

5. It was the principle / principal of the issue that bothered him.

6. We had to swim in our clothes because we forgot hour / our bathing suits!

7. Before the play, I practiced saying my lines aloud / allowed.

8. My uncle put some oil in the hinges so the door won't creek / creak.

9. A whale can be the sighs / size of a school bus.

10. The beavers were busy building a dam across the creek / creak.

Blank Out!

FILL IN the blanks with keywords.

aloud	allowed	creak	creek	hour
our	principal	principle	sighs	size

1. The _____ tells how big or small something is.

2. This word describes something you believe is right. _____

3. If it's your pizza *and* my pizza, it's _____ pizza.

4. When you're permitted to do something, you're _____ to do it.

5. When someone speaks above a whisper, he's speaking _____.

6. The sounds of people exhaling loudly are called _____.

7. A _____ is smaller than a stream.

8. The head of a school is the _____.

9. This word is the sound a rocking chair sometimes makes. _____

10. It takes an _____ for the minute hand to go around the clock once.

 Check It!

Cut out the Check It! section on page 131, and see if you got the answers right.

3

Keywords

ad•dress¹—uh-DREHS *verb* 1. to speak about an issue 2. to deal with

ad•dress²—A-drehs *noun* information that gives the location of someone's home or business or e-mail account

ex•cuse¹—ihk-SKYOOS *noun* an explanation given to obtain forgiveness

ex•cuse²—ihk-SKYOOZ *verb* to overlook or forgive

proj•ect¹—PRAH-jehkt *noun* a task

proj•ect²—pruh-JEHKT *verb* 1. to forecast 2. to jut out 3. to say loudly

re•cord¹—REHK-erd *noun* 1. something official that preserves knowledge or history 2. best performance or greatest achievement

re•cord²—ri-KORD *verb* to make an audio, video, or written account of something

wound¹—woond *noun* an injury

wound²—wownd *verb* 1. wrapped around something 2. changed direction

 **Check It!**

Page 140

Read & Replace

1. project
2. address
3. record
4. wound
5. wound
6. excuse
7. project

Page 141

Homograph Hopscotch

1. excuse
2. record
3. wound

Page 142

Write It Right

1. wound
2. project
3. Excuse
4. address
5. record
Riddle: carpet

Page 143

Criss Cross

ACROSS	DOWN
2. address	1. record
3. project	4. record
7. project	5. excuse
8. wound	6. address
9. excuse	8. wound

Homographs

 Check It!

Page 144

Blank Out!

1. project
2. address
3. record
4. record
5. wound
6. excuse
7. address
8. wound
9. project
10. excuse

Page 145

Double Match Up

1. a, f
2. e, k
3. b, h
4. l, n
5. c, i
6. j, m
7. d, g

Page 146

Blank Out!

1. project
2. record
3. wound
4. address
5. excuse
6. address
7. Project
8. excuse
9. record
10. wound

Read & Replace

HOMOGRAPHS are words that have the same spelling but different meanings. They can sound alike or not, like *tear* that you cry and a *tear* in a page.

READ the list. FILL IN the blanks with keywords.

Seven Outrageous Excuses

Did you ever get invited somewhere you really didn't want to go? Just pick an excuse from this handy list!

1. I don't need to water the garden. I _____ a big summer snow storm any minute.

2. I tried to run the errand for you, Mom, but an alien swiped the _____.

3. I couldn't practice the piano because I was trying to set a _____ for watching TV.

4. I'd eat those beets, but my allergy to red food makes me dizzy, and I might fall and _____ myself.

5. Sorry I missed practice, but my brother _____ me up with string and rolled me under the bed, and I was trapped until my mom found me.

6. You'll have to _____ me—it's time for my daily chicken dance.

7. I wasn't yelling—I was just trying to _____ so they could hear me on the moon.

Homograph Hopscotch

LOOK AT the definitions in each hopscotch board. FILL IN the matching keyword at the top of the board.

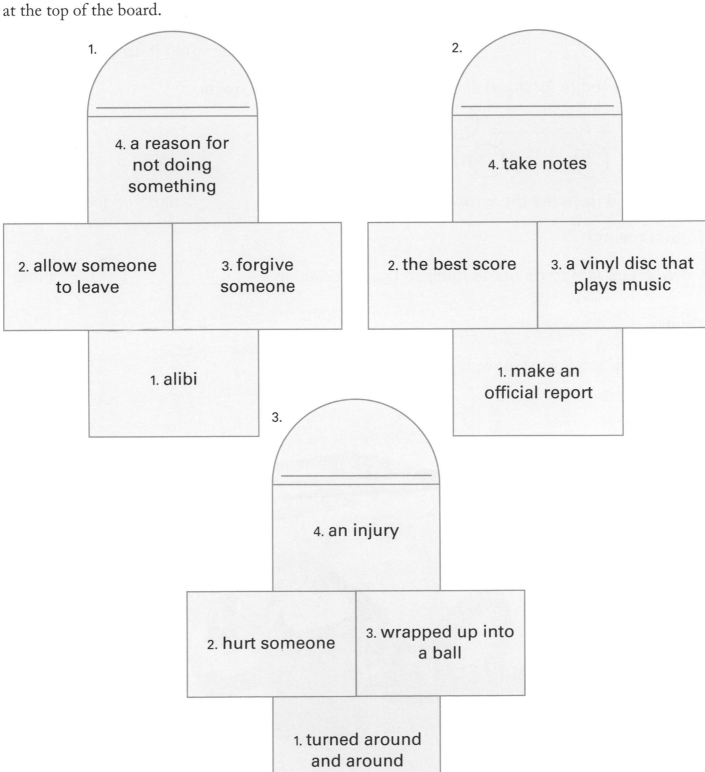

1.

4. a reason for not doing something

2. allow someone to leave

3. forgive someone

1. alibi

2.

4. take notes

2. the best score

3. a vinyl disc that plays music

1. make an official report

3.

4. an injury

2. hurt someone

3. wrapped up into a ball

1. turned around and around

Write It Right

FILL IN the blanks by answering the clues with keywords. Then UNSCRAMBLE the letters in the circles to answer the riddle.

1. After I ___ ___ ___ ___ ___ the yarn into a ball, my cat tangled it up again!

2. My dad tried to fix the sink quickly but it turned into a major
   (○) ___ ___ ___ ___ (○) .

3. "___ ___ (○) ___ ___ (○) me!" I said after I burped.

4. My friend gave me the wrong (○) ___ ___ ___ ___ ___ ___ , and I ended up in the next town!

5. I woke up late to go to the mall, so I got dressed in ___ ___ ___ ___ (○)___ time.

Riddle

What goes up and down stairs without moving? ___ ___ ___ ___ ___ ___

Criss Cross

FILL IN the grid by answering the clues with keywords. Each keyword is used twice, with two different pronunciations.

ACROSS

2. What you write on an envelope

3. A big task

7. How to make yourself heard

8. Wrapped around

9. Let someone leave the dinner table

DOWN

1. Make an audio copy

4. The biggest or best achievement

5. "My homework flew out of the bus window."

6. Speak to a crowd

8. A bruise or cut

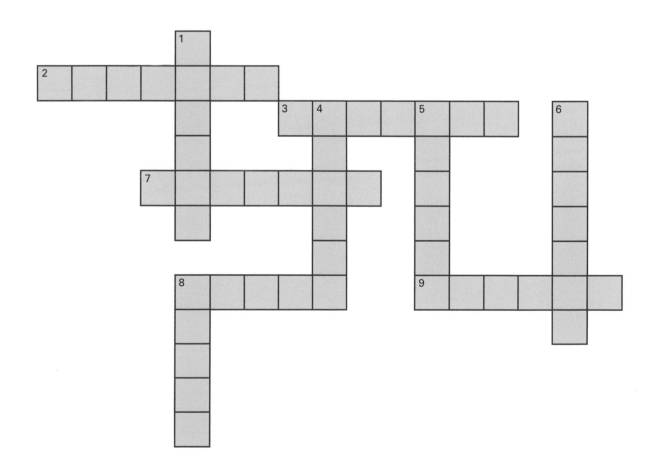

Blank Out!

FILL in the blanks with keywords.

address	excuse	project	record	wound

1. We decided to build a clubhouse for our next big _____.

2. Naomi got the _____ for the roller rink from the phone book.

3. Carlos broke the team _____ for goals scored in one game.

4. My mom keeps a chart to _____ the chores I do each week.

5. Madeline noticed a _____ on her dog's left paw.

6. There's no _____ for rude behavior!

7. The president is going to _____ the nation shortly.

8. When my sister was done flying her kite, she _____ the string on the spool.

9. Zack used a laptop to _____ the movie onto a screen.

10. My coach said he would _____ me from practice because I was sick.

Double Match Up

LOOK AT the words. FILL IN the blanks with the letters for both meanings of each word.

1. bark   _____   _____

2. bow   _____   _____

3. dove   _____   _____

4. tear   _____   _____

5. lead   _____   _____

6. sewer   _____   _____

7. wind   _____   _____

a. the noise a dog makes

b. jumped head first

c. a kind of heavy metal

d. air that blows

e. loops formed when a ribbon is tied

f. outer surface of a tree

g. wrap something around

h. a bird of peace

i. to show the way

j. pipes in the ground that carry waste

k. a tool used when playing a violin

l. a drop formed when crying

m. someone who stitches

n. rip

Blank Out!

FILL in the blanks with keywords.

| address | excuse | project | record | wound |

1. Every time my sister cooks, the kitchen looks like a giant science _____.

2. James is trying to set a world _____ for the longest burp.

3. I took a header into a bush on my skateboard and got the grossest knee _____ ever. Yes!

4. My uncle Ira is such a dork—his e-mail _____ is hey@whatsamatteryou.com.

5. "The dog ate my homework" is the oldest _____ in the world.

6. Quit making such a fuss—you're not giving the Gettysburg _____ you know!

7. Poor Toby, everybody could hear his mother backstage telling him, "_____ your voice, Poopsie."

8. Well, _____ me for living!

9. My dad has no idea how to work the DVR, so I have to _____ all his faves for him.

10. Snoop wasn't laughing and joking with the rest of the team in the locker room because he's _____ too tight.

✓ Check It!

Cut out the Check It! section on page 139, and see if you got the answers right.

Just Right!

You've learned a lot of words so far. Are you ready to have some fun with them?

Synonyms may have similar meanings, but it's important to know which one is the right one to use in a situation. READ each sentence. Then CIRCLE the synonym that best fits the sentence.

1. Annie would rather go to the movie with a buddy / ally than by herself.

2. After a hard day at the office, my mom likes to loosen up / relax.

3. Over the summer, Nicki learned to dive / plunge off the board.

4. My brother won't enable / allow me to use his new baseball glove.

5. I hope we never stop / discontinue being friends.

6. It is polite / respectful to say "thank you" when you receive a gift.

Seesaw

LOOK AT the seesaws. WRITE a synonym on the level seesaws. Write an antonym on the slanted seesaws.

1. likely _____ ▲

3. tiny _____ ▲

2. prevent _____ ▲

4. smart _____ ▲

Check It!

Page 147

Just Right!

1. buddy   4. allow
2. relax   5. stop
3. dive   6. polite

Seesaw

1. probably
2. enable
3. immense
4. intelligent

Page 148

Word Search

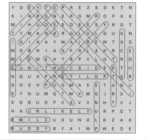

Page 149

Fixer Upper

Glossary: 3. principal
1. allowed   4. size
2. hour   5. creek

Double Trouble

1. to speak to a crowd
2. an explanation for something you shouldn't have done
3. a task
4. to write an historic account
5. wrapped around

Page 150

Sniglets!

1. pieoneer
2. e-male
3. bowling bawl
4. underwhere
5. saleboat
6. supersighs

Word Search

CIRCLE all of the words in the word grid. Words go across, up, down, or diagonally.

amuse	polite	buddy	probably
discontinue	enable	immense	plunge
relax	climb	prevent	enemy
bore	rude	start	stupid
tiny	unlikely	stress	intelligent

```
Y  D  E  Y  T  E  P  R  E  Z  S  D  K  T  N
K  I  N  R  S  N  E  R  O  M  R  O  F  X  K
M  I  H  U  O  E  E  D  E  E  S  Y  R  O  T
T  Y  M  A  N  B  R  G  L  V  L  D  U  S  N
I  A  I  A  A  Y  W  A  I  B  E  W  T  S  D
M  O  B  H  I  A  X  E  A  L  Z  N  R  E  E
M  L  D  W  E  H  T  B  P  V  L  G  T  R  D
E  U  N  I  T  N  O  C  S  I  D  E  S  T  U
N  Q  U  X  P  R  E  T  I  L  O  P  T  S  R
S  N  S  H  P  U  Q  M  A  K  E  T  A  N  U
E  Y  N  U  M  Q  T  M  Y  M  G  J  R  S  I
K  D  B  U  D  P  C  S  V  V  N  H  T  V  J
H  A  U  N  L  I  K  E  L  Y  U  R  P  D  T
B  M  I  L  C  U  X  U  N  O  L  K  Z  A  X
B  U  D  D  Y  B  F  A  I  W  P  W  E  O  E
```

Fixer Upper

Our homophones have gotten all mixed up. READ the glossary. WRITE the keyword homophone that matches the definition.

Glossary

aloud: was given permission

our: unit of time; 60 minutes

principle: the main leader

sighs: how large something is height times width

creak: a small stream

1. _____

2. _____

3. _____

4. _____

5. _____

Double Trouble

WRITE another meaning for each homograph.

address: where something is located OR

excuse: let someone go OR

project: speak loudly OR

record: the highest or best ever OR

wound: to injure OR

1. _____

2. _____

3. _____

4. _____

5. _____

Sniglets!

Would you like to make up a new word? You can start by making up a *sniglet*. Sniglets are fun-sounding words that use pieces of existing words. Here are some homophone sniglets:

bowling bawl—a crying fit in a bowling alley
supersighs—loud exhaling sounds you make when you're frustrated
e-male—a computer note from a boy or man
pieoneer—one of the first people to eat a piece of pie
saleboat—a good price on a sea vessel
underwhere–missing undergarments

WRITE a sniglet from the list to complete each sentence.

1. When dessert was served, I volunteered to be the _____.

2. Sarah was excited when Abel, captain of the football team, sent her

   an _____.

3. After three gutter balls, my brother had a _____.

4. All I have is _____, so I can't get dressed and go with you.

5. My mother saved money by buying my dad a second-hand _____ for

   his birthday.

6. You should've heard the waiter's _____ when we changed our order

   for the third time.

 **Check It!**

Cut out Check It! to see if you got the answers right.

Keywords

im•po•lite—IHM-puh-LIT *adjective* 1. rude 2. lacking good manners

im•pos•si•ble—ihm-PAHS-uh-buhl *adjective* not able to occur

in•com•plete—ihn-kuhm-PLEET *adjective* not having all the necessary parts

in•cor•rect—ihn-kuh-REHKT *adjective* not having the right information

mis•be•have—MIHS-bih-HAYV *verb* to fail to act properly

mis•treat—mihs-TREET *verb* to deal with someone unfairly or cruelly

mis•un•der•stand—MIHS-uhn-der-STAND *verb* to fail to interpret something correctly

trans•con•ti•nen•tal—TRANZ-kahn-tuh-NEHN-tuhl *adjective* crossing a continent

trans•late—TRANZ-layt *verb* to convert one language to another

trans•port—tranz-PORT *verb* to carry from one place to another

✓ Check It!

Page 152

Match Up

impossible, i
incomplete, f
incorrect, e
misbehave, g
mistreat, a
misunderstand, d
transcontinental, b
translate, h
transport, c

Page 153

Read & Replace

1. impolite
2. misbehave
3. mistreat

Bonus:
"Not My Favorite"
"That's why you're not my fave."

Page 154

Petal Power

1. mis
2. in
3. trans
4. im

Page 155

Stack Up

IN: edible, exact, sane, humane
IM: perfect, mature
MIS: pronounce, inform
TRANS: atlantic, plant

 **Check It!**

Page 156

Criss Cross

Across
3. mistreat
4. incomplete
6. translate
7. impossible

Down
1. transcontinental
2. impolite
4. incorrect
5. transport

Page 157

Blank Out!

1. transcontinental
2. incorrect
3. misbehave
4. impolite
5. mistreat
6. translate
7. misunderstand
8. incomplete
9. impossible
10. transport

Page 158

Blank Out!

1. incomplete
2. transport
3. impolite
4. misbehave
5. misunderstand
6. incorrect
7. impossible
8. mistreat
9. transcontinental
10. translate

Match Up

A PREFIX is a group of letters that comes at the beginning of a word. Each prefix has its own meaning. When you know the meaning of the prefix, you can often figure out the meaning of the word.

MATCH the prefixes in the box to the roots. WRITE each word and then MATCH it to its definition.

HINT: You can use each prefix more than once.

in-/im- = not   mis- = bad   trans- = across

port _____ ____

understand _____ ____

late _____ ____

continental _____ ____

correct _____ ____

possible _____ ____

treat _____ ____

behave _____ ____

complete _____ ____

Definitions:
a. to deal with someone unfairly or cruelly
b. crossing a continent
c. to carry from one place to another
d. to fail to interpret something correctly
e. not having the right information
f. not having all the necessary parts
g. to fail to act properly
h. to convert one language to another
i. not able to occur

Read & Replace

READ the poem. Then FILL IN the blanks in the second poem using keywords to give the poem the opposite meaning.

My Favorite

You're ever so **polite**,

And you always **behave**,

You know how to **treat** me.

That's why you're my fave!

My Favorite

You're ever so 1_____,

And you always 2_____,

You know how to 3_____ me.

That's why you're my fave!

BONUS!

For the second poem, what word do you need to add to the last line to make it make sense? Add that extra word to the title and last line.

Petal Power

READ the roots on the petals around each flower. FILL IN the center of each flower with a prefix that could go with all of its roots.

1.

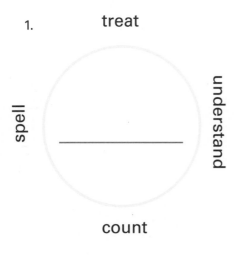

treat

spell

understand

count

2.

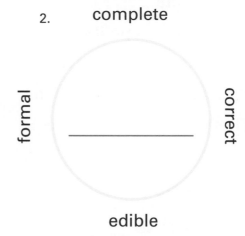

complete

formal

correct

edible

3.

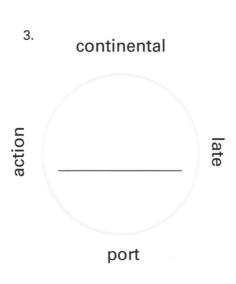

continental

action

late

port

4.

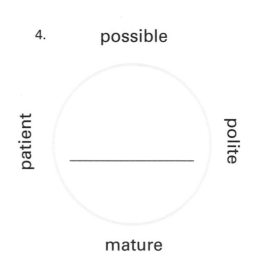

possible

patient

polite

mature

Stack Up

LOOK AT the root words in the box. MATCH them with prefixes to make new words. WRITE the new words under each prefix.

| sane | pronounce | exact | plant | mature |
| humane | atlantic | perfect | inform | edible |

in-

_____

_____

_____

_____

im-

_____

_____

mis-

_____

_____

trans-

_____

_____

Criss Cross

FILL IN the grid by answering the clues with keywords.

ACROSS

3. Handle someone badly
4. Not finished
6. Change words to a different language
7. Can't be done

DOWN

1. From coast to coast
2. Rude
4. Wrong
5. Carry

Blank Out!

FILL IN the blanks with keywords.

1. The _____ railroad runs across the entire country.

2. Lily said she thought I liked Bryan, but I told her she was totally

   _____.

3. If we leave our dog alone too long, he tends to _____.

4. I said I liked her gift because I didn't want to be _____.

5. People who _____ animals should not be allowed to have pets.

6. The story was in Spanish so I got my friend to _____ it.

7. If you don't listen closely, you might _____ the directions.

8. The jigsaw puzzle was _____ because our dog ate a piece!

9. My sister packed so much that it was _____ to close her suitcase.

10. We needed a big truck and some movers to _____ the piano to

    our house.

Blank Out!

FILL IN the blanks with keywords.

1. The story is incomplete because the last few pages are _____.

2. You _____ something to get it from one place to another.

3. Someone who doesn't have good manners is _____.

4. Some kids _____ when their parents are out.

5. A person who isn't listening closely might _____.

6. A wrong answer is _____.

7. Something that just can't be done is _____.

8. You can't borrow my clothes anymore because you always _____ them.

9. A highway stretching coast to coast is _____.

10. To read a book in another language, you might _____ it.

Keywords

an•ti•bac•te•ri•al—AN-tee-bak-TEER-ee-uhl *adjective* active in killing germs

an•ti•slav•er•y—AN-tee-SLAY-vuh-ree *adjective* against the practice of owning people

an•ti•so•cial—AN-tee-SOH-shuhl *adjective* not wanting to be with other people

in•ter•na•tion•al—IHN-ter-NASH-uh-nuhl *adjective* between two or more countries

in•ter•sect—IHN-ter-SEHKT *verb* 1. to divide something by going across it 2. to cross or overlap

in•ter•state—IHN-ter-stayt *adjective* between two or more states

mul•ti•col•ored—MUHL-tih-KUHL-erd *adjective* having many hues

mul•ti•cul•tur•al—MUHL-tee-KUHL-cher-uhl *adjective* reflecting many different customs and backgrounds

mul•ti•mil•lion•aire—MUHL-tee-MIHL-yuh-NEHR *noun* someone a person who has millions of dollars

mul•ti•pur•pose—MUHL-tee-PER-puhs *adjective* having more than one use

✓ Check It!

Page 160
Read & Replace

1. multipurpose
2. intersect
3. interstate
4. multimillionaire
5. antibacterial
6. antisocial
7. multicolored
8. international
9. multicultural
10. antislavery

Page 161
Petal Power

1. inter
2. anti
3. multi

Bonus:
predawn
pregame
preheat
preteen

Page 162
Tic-Tac-Toe

1. war, gravity, bodies
2. galactic, weave, action
3. layer, task, channel

antibodies
anticlimax
antigravity
antivenom
antiwar

interaction
interchangeable
intergalactic
international
interweave

multichannel
multifaceted
multilayer
multilingual
multitask

More Prefixes

 **Check It!**

Page 163

Criss Cross

Across
3. intersect
6. antislavery
7. antisocial

Down
1. multicultural
2. interstate
4. international
5. multicolored

Page 164

Blank Out!

1. multimillionaire
2. international
3. multicultural
4. antislavery
5. antibacterial
6. multipurpose
7. intersect
8. multicolored
9. antisocial
10. interstate

Page 165

It's Puzzling!

antifreeze
antiwar
intercom
interlocked
interview
multiethnic
multiplex
multiplication

Page 166

Blank Out!

1. interstate
2. multicolored
3. antisocial
4. multimillionaire
5. antibacterial
6. antislavery
7. multicultural
8. international
9. intersect
10. multipurpose

Read & Replace

READ the newspaper story. FILL IN the blanks with keywords.

HINT: Make sure to read the whole story first.

anti- = against   inter- = among or between   multi = many or much

INVENTION CONVENTION

This year's Invention Convention entries were zany. Michael Finch created the "Umbre-Light-Chair," a 1_____ item—an umbrella, flashlight, and folding chair. He explained that the three purposes would 2_____ if you wanted to sit on the beach on a rainy night. "I hope to win the local convention and go to the 3_____ competition, he said. "One day I'll be a 4_____!"

Lydia Nelson is a germ freak. She created 5_____ lip balm. "Any germs that touch your lips are killed before they enter your mouth." She added that it's best to avoid large groups of people, "without being too 6_____."

First prize went to Alex Price. He created a 7_____ symbol with different paints. "I would like my design to become an 8_____ symbol of respect so people can honor our 9_____ world." He added, "I read about the efforts people made during the 10_____ movement to gain freedom. This is something we can use today."

Petal Power

READ the roots on the petals around each flower. FILL IN the center of each flower with a prefix that could go with all of its roots.

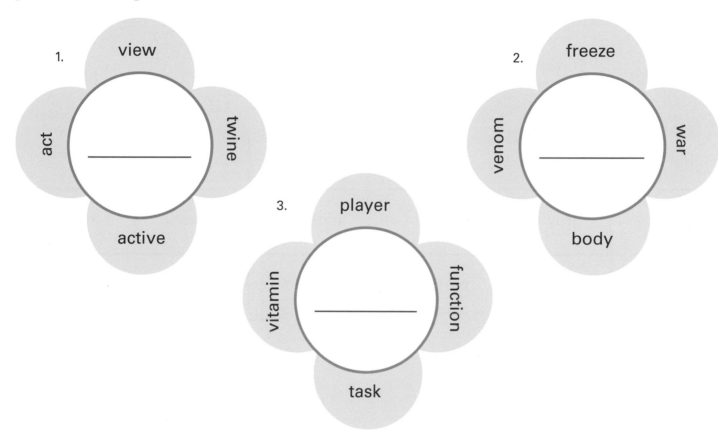

1.

view

act

twine

_____

active

2.

freeze

venom

war

_____

body

3.

player

vitamin

function

_____

task

BONUS!

Now you try it! The prefix in the middle of this flower means *before*. FILL IN the petals with root words that go with the center. One petal is filled in for you!

| bend | dawn | game | teen |
| circle | feet | heat | obey |

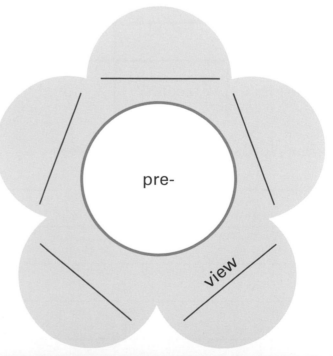

pre-

view

Tic-Tac-Toe

PLAY Tic-tac-toe with prefixes. CIRCLE any root that could be used with the prefix in blue. PUT an X through any word that could not be used with the prefix. When you find three X's or O's in a row, you're a winner! The line can go across, down, or diagonally. When you're done, make a list of all the new words.

HINT: If you find a word you don't know, check a dictionary or thesaurus.

1. anti

paper	war	happy
index	gravity	climax
venom	bodies	planets

2. inter

changeable	car	action
addition	weave	national
galactic	spoke	mud

3. multi

layer	green	porch
task	travel	lingual
channel	faceted	novel

Other Words Created with Prefixes

_____

_____

_____

_____

Criss Cross

FILL IN the grid by answering the clues with keywords.

ACROSS

3. Divide by running across something

6. Against the ownership of people

7. Not interested in hanging out

DOWN

1. From many different backgrounds

2. The champions traveled 200 miles to an _____ competition.

4. Flights to other countries depart from the _____ terminal.

5. Not just one hue

Blank Out!

FILL IN the blanks with keywords.

1. The inventor of the Pet Rock probably became a _____.

2. With their new hit song in many different languages, the band became an _____ sensation.

3. My friends and I prepared a _____ feast with foods from different backgrounds.

4. Harriet Tubman was a famous leader of the _____ movement.

5. Mary is such a germ freak that she applies _____ gel every time she shakes hands with someone.

6. Zach's crazy _____ tool had a screwdriver, file, scissors, nail clippers, tongue scraper, and ear wax remover!

7. On a globe, lines of latitude and longitude _____ each other.

8. She took out all her markers to make a _____ poster.

9. Alison didn't want to go to the party because she was feeling _____.

10. To get from Pennsylvania to Ohio, we took an _____ highway.

It's Puzzling!

MATCH each prefix to a root. Then WRITE the words in the blanks.

HINT: You can use the same prefix more than once.

multi-

anti-

inter-

ethnic

war

freeze

plication

locked

com

plex

view

_____

_____

_____

_____

_____

_____

_____

Blank Out!

FILL IN the blanks with keywords.

1. When we left on vacation, we took the _____ highway to the airport.

2. A rainbow is _____.

3. Someone who prefers to be alone is _____.

4. A person with loads of money may be a _____.

5. Something that kills germs is _____.

6. A movement against some people owning other people is _____.

7. A group with people from many backgrounds is _____.

8. A world's fair is an _____ event.

9. Two lines that cross each other _____.

10. Something that has many uses is _____.

Keywords

bi•an•nu•al—bi-AN-yoo-uhl *adjective* occurring twice a year

bi•cy•cle—BI-sihk-uhl *noun* a two-wheeled vehicle

bin•oc•u•lars—buh-NAHK-yuh-lerz *noun* a magnifying device with two lenses for seeing faraway objects

tri•an•gle—TRI-ang-guhl *noun* a shape with three sides

tri•ath•lon—tri-ATH-luhn *noun* a sports event with three different activities

trip•lets—TRIHP-lihts *noun* three children born at the same birth

tri•pod—TRI-pahd *noun* a three-legged stand

u•ni•corn—YOO-nih-korn *noun* an imaginary horse-like animal with a single horn

u•ni•cy•cle—YOO-nih-SI-kuhl *noun* a one-wheeled vehicle

u•ni•verse—YOO-nuh-vers *noun* all planets, space, matter, and energy in one whole

---

✓ Check It!

Page 168
Read & Replace

1. unicycle
2. bicycle
3. binoculars
4. unicorn
5. triplets
6. triangle
7. tripod
8. triathlon
9. biannual
10. universe

Page 169
1, 2, 3 Stack Up!

1. unicorn, unicycle, universe
2. bicycle, binoculars, biannual
3. triangle, tripod, triathlon, triplets

Page 170
Tic-Tac-Toe

1. uniform, unibrow, unicolor
2. bipolar, biweekly, bimonthly
3. triathlete, tricolor, tricycle

uniform
unibrow
unicorn
unicolor
unidirectional

bifocals
bilevel
bipolar
biweekly
bimonthly

trifocal
trifold
triathlete
tricolor
tricycle

Read & Replace

Some prefixes just add a number to the root word. A *uni*cycle has one wheel. A *bi*cycle has two wheels. And a *tri*cycle has three wheels.

READ the story. FILL IN the blanks with keywords.

Prefix Meanings: *uni- = one   bi- = two   tri- = three*

unicorn	unicycle	universe	bicycle
binoculars	binannual	triangle	tripod
triathlon	triplets		

Every year my town has a festival. This year was the best ever.

A clown juggled while riding a 1_____.

I can't ride one even when I'm *not* juggling! It was even more amazing to see an elephant riding a 2_____!

I looked at it up-close through my 3_____. A horse was dressed in a costume as a 4_____. Three acrobats were identical 5_____. They swung from a giant 6_____. A photographer had a camera on a 7_____. You could get your picture taken behind silly cardboard cutouts. Afterwards, kids and grown-ups could join in a 8_____ contest with wheelbarrow races, sack hops, and leapfrog! It only happens once a year, but I wish it were a 9_____ event. It's the best festival in the 10_____!

1, 2, 3 Stack Up!

READ the definitions. Then WRITE the keyword under the number that matches its prefix.

An animal with one horn

Happening twice a year

A stand with three legs

A set of three babies born at the same time

The whole world and beyond

A vehicle with two wheels

A shape with three angles

A magnifying device with two lenses

A sports event with three different activities

A vehicle with one wheel

1	2	3
_____	_____	_____
_____	_____	_____
_____	_____	_____

Tic-Tac-Toe

PLAY Tic-tac-toe with prefixes. CIRCLE any root that could be used with the prefix in blue. PUT an X through any word that could not be used with the prefix. When you find three Xs or Os in a row, you're a winner! The line can go across, down, or diagonally. When you're done, make a list of all the words.

HINT: If you find a word you don't know, check a dictionary or thesaurus.

1. uni

week	month	corn
form	brow	color
stream	directional	change

2. bi

polar	tail	pack
level	weekly	grain
cell	focals	monthly

3. tri

focal	athlete	student
notes	color	fold
elbow	cycle	phone

Other Words Created with Prefixes

_____

_____

_____

_____

Criss Cross

FILL IN the grid by answering the clues with keywords.

ACROSS

5. Bicycle minus one wheel

6. Something steady to put your camera on

7. One more than twins

DOWN

1. A unicycle plus one wheel

2. What you might use to watch birds

3. Mythical one-horned creature

4. A simple instrument to ding in music class

5. Something greater than our galaxy

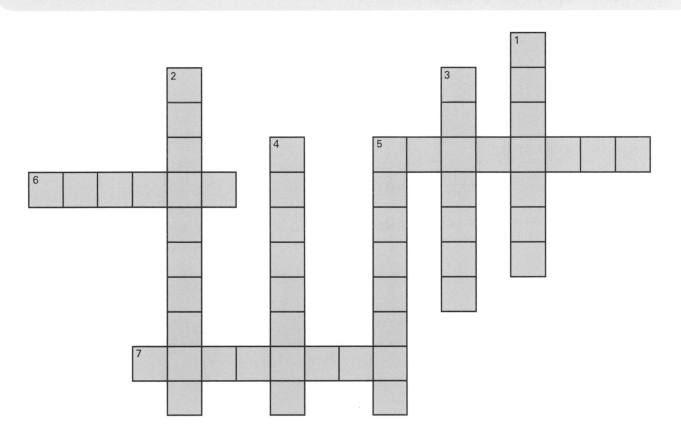

Blank Out!

FILL IN the blanks with keywords.

1. Riding a _____ is great exercise.

2. Dad was training to push a shopping cart up a hill and balance a dozen eggs on his head for the grocery _____.

3. Our neighborhood throws a _____ block party in the spring and fall.

4. My little sister won't go anywhere without her stuffed _____.

5. A slice of pizza is shaped like a _____.

6. Each planet is one little speck in the _____.

7. I crouched by the window and used _____ to try to catch the newspaper thief.

8. For the talent show, Tim rode his _____ while balancing his cat George on one hand.

9. Our dog only has three legs, so we named him _____.

10. The _____ played tricks on their teachers by switching places.

Name It!

LOOK AT the pictures. INVENT a word that describes the picture, using the prefixes *uni-*, *bi-*, and *tri-*. WRITE the word and define it.

1. _____

_____

_____

2. _____

_____

_____

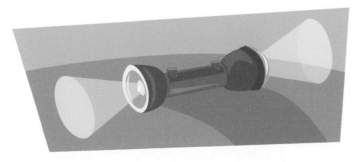

3. _____

_____

_____

Blank Out!

FILL IN the blanks with keywords.

1. _____ can help you watch a baseball game from the bleachers.

2. A _____ is a shape with three sides.

3. A _____ is an environmentally friendly way to get around.

4. A clown sometimes rides a _____.

5. A _____ can be an event with biking, running, and swimming.

6. The _____ is even bigger than the solar system.

7. This word describes something that happens twice a year. _____

8. A _____ is a mythical creature.

9. A three-legged stool is a _____.

10. Three babies delivered at the same birth are _____.

Keywords

cer•tain•ty—SER-tuhn-tee *noun* the state of being sure

con•struc•tion—kuhn-STRUHK-shuhn *noun* the process of building

cre•a•tive—kree-AY-tihv *adjective* capable of making or imagining new things

de•ci•sive—dih-SI-sihv *adjective* having the power to make firm decisions

ed•u•ca•tion—EH-juh-KAY-shuhn *noun* the act of learning or teaching

ex•plo•sion—ihk-SPLOH-zhuhn *noun* a sudden burst, often loud or violent

i•mag•i•na•tion—ih-MAJ-uh-NAY-shuhn *noun* the ability of the mind to create

in•for•ma•tion—IHN-fer-MAY-shuhn *noun* facts or knowledge gained from any source

per•mis•sion—per-MIH-shuhn *noun* the act of allowing

sim•i•lar•i•ty—SIHM-uh-LAR-ih-tee *noun* the state of having a lot in common

✓ Check It!

Page 176

Read & Replace

1. construction
2. imagination
3. information
4. creative
5. similarity
6. explosion
7. permission
8. decisive
9. certainty
10. education

Page 177

Suffix Hopscotch

1. -ion
2. -ity
3. -ive

Page 178

Match Up

1. deletion
2. royalty
3. conversation
4. revision
5. frailty

Page 179

Criss Cross

ACROSS	DOWN
4. construction	1. education
7. imagination	2. similarity
8. permission	3. creative
	5. decisive
	6. explosion

Suffixes

Read & Replace

READ the diary entry. FILL IN the blanks with keywords.

Stadium Blast!

Today they started 1_____ on the new baseball

stadium. I've been to the old arena many times. The idea of

building an entirely new one boggled my 2_____.

How would they do it? I found some 3_____

online. The designs for the new stadium are very

4_____. There will be a giant dolphin-shaped

scoreboard past the outfield fence. There will be brand-new,

fancy dugouts. The only 5_____ will be the field!

My dad told me that they were going to start by demolishing

the old structure. They were actually going to set off an

6_____! Dad said that people had

7_____ to watch from a safe distance. He asked if

I wanted to go. Naturally, I replied with a 8_____

YES!

Even though we were across the street, the blast was deafening.

The buildings around us shook. The stadium came crashing

down. One thing I can say with 9_____—it was

an 10_____!

Check It!

Page 180

Blank Out!

1. education
2. decisive
3. construction
4. information
5. explosion
6. certainty
7. permission
8. creative
9. similarity
10. imagination

Page 181

Chopping Block

1. combine
2. invade
3. tense
4. loyal
5. migrate
6. opt
7. illustrate
8. invade
9. add
10. divide

Page 182

Blank Out!

1. permission
2. Construction
3. explosion
4. decisive
5. similarity
6. creative
7. imagination
8. information
9. Certainty
10. Education

Suffix Hopscotch

LOOK AT the root words in each hopscotch board. FILL IN the matching suffix at the top of the board.

HINT: Sometimes you drop or change a letter from the root word when you add the suffix.

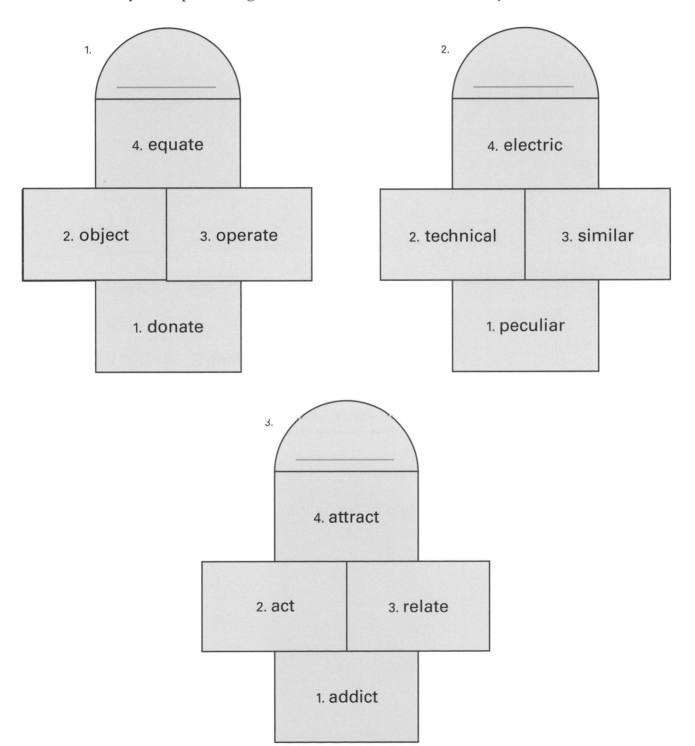

1.

_____

4. equate

2. object   3. operate

1. donate

2.

_____

4. electric

2. technical   3. similar

1. peculiar

3.

_____

4. attract

2. act   3. relate

1. addict

Match Up

MATCH each root to a suffix. Then WRITE the word next to its definition.

HINT: Sometimes you drop or change a letter from the root word when you add the suffix.

Root	Suffix
delete	-ty
royal	-ion
converse	-ion
revise	-ty
frail	-ation

	Word	Definition
1.	_____	the act of removing something
2.	_____	kings, queens, and their relatives
3.	_____	discussion
4.	_____	a changed form of something
5.	_____	the state of being weak or delicate

Criss Cross

FILL IN the grid by answering the clues with keywords.

ACROSS

4. Describes a zone where people wear hardhats

7. Something you need to think up a great plan

8. The go-ahead

DOWN

1. Something you get from school

2. A likeness or resemblance

3. Comes up with zany ideas

5. No trouble choosing

6. Something that goes BOOM!

Blank Out!

FILL IN the blanks with keywords.

certainty	construction	creative	education	decisive
explosion	imagination	information	permission	similarity

1. I tried to convince my mom the rock concert would further my musical

   _____, but she still wouldn't let me go.

2. When it was time to choose between chocolate cake and apple pie, Lila

   was _____.

3. The mall was closed for new _____.

4. Madeline is like a walking _____ booth. She knows everything

   about everyone.

5. During the fireworks, one _____ really scared my dog.

6. Lucy picked out her outfit with great _____.

7. Ingrid's mom granted us _____ to go on the roller coaster.

8. Aaron's art teacher was impressed with his _____ painting.

9. There is a lot of _____ between soccer and football, but they are not

   exactly the same.

10. The science fiction writer had

    an amazing _____.

Chopping Block

READ the words. CHOP OFF the suffix in each word by drawing a line right before the ending. WRITE the root word in the blank.

HINT: You may have to add a letter or two to make the root word.

1. c o m b i n a t i o n _____

2. i n v a s i o n _____

3. t e n s i o n _____

4. l o y a l t y _____

5. m i g r a t i o n _____

6. o p t i o n _____

7. i l l u s t r a t i o n _____

8. i n v a s i v e _____

9. a d d i t i v e _____

10. d i v i s i v e _____

Blank Out!

FILL IN the blanks with keywords.

1. You need _____ to borrow your friend's bike.

2. _____ is the process of creating a new building, for example.

3. When two chemicals mix, there could be an _____.

4. Someone who knows exactly what she wants is _____.

5. Twins usually share more than one _____.

6. Someone who shows originality and cleverness is _____.

7. You need to use your _____ to dream up new ideas.

8. You get _____ from an encyclopedia.

9. _____ is knowing something without doubt.

10. _____ is the result of instruction, training, or study.

Keywords

au•di•ble—AW-duh-buhl *adjective* able to be heard

be•liev•a•ble—bih-LEE-vuh-buhl *adjective* can be considered true

co•lo•ni•al—kuh-LOH-nee-uhl *adjective* referring to the 13 British colonies that became the United States of America

com•fort•a•ble—KUHM-fer-tuh-buhl *adjective* a state of well-being or ease

log•i•cal—LAHJ-ih-kuhl *adjective* resulting from clear thinking

me•tal•lic—muh-TAL-ihk *adjective* made of or containing metal

mu•si•cal—MYOO-zih-kuhl *adjective* having a natural ability to carry a tune or play an instrument

no•tice•a•ble—NOH-tih-suh-buhl *adjective* can be easily observed

po•et•ic—poh-EHT-ihk *adjective* 1. having a rhyming or lyrical quality 2. pleasing to the ear

re•vers•i•ble—rih-VER-suh-buhl *adjective* 1. able to be turned back 2. can be worn inside out

✓ Check It!

Page 184

Read & Replace

1. comfortable
2. audible
3. noticeable
4. metallic
5. musical
6. poetic
7. reversible
8. logical
9. believable
10. colonial

Page 185

Suffix Hopscotch

1. –ic
2. –able
3. -al

Page 186

Match Up

1. official
2. chewable
3. disposable
4. heroic
5. reliable

Page 187

Criss Cross

ACROSS	DOWN
1. colonial	1. comfortable
6. reversible	2. noticeable
7. audible	3. poetic
8. logical	4. musical
9. believable	5. metallic

More Suffixes

 Check It!

Page 188

Blank Out!

1. audible
2. noticeable
3. musical
4. comfortable
5. believable
6. reversible
7. logical
8. colonial
9. poetic
10. metallic

Page 189

Chopping Block

1. mistake
2. sense
3. history
4. melody
5. optic
6. teach
7. robot
8. volcano
9. remove
10. value

Page 190

Blank Out!

1. logical
2. musical
3. colonial
4. audible
5. reversible
6. poetic
7. noticeable
8. metallic
9. comfortable
10. believable

Read & Replace

READ the story FILL IN the blanks with keywords.

Time Travel

Wendy and her family boarded the plane. She couldn't wait to see her grandparents in Massachusetts. She adjusted her seat to get 1_____. The flight attendant's microphone was off, so her speech was not 2_____. Wendy put her hand near her ear in a 3_____ gesture, and the flight attendant turned on her microphone, and showed how to click the 4_____ seat buckle into place.

Wendy hooked her headphone into the armrest. There was one 5_____ station with songs from her parents' era. Then there was a station with Shakespeare's sonnets and other 6_____ readings. Thankfully, they began to show a movie. It was about a time machine. Since people could go back in time, their mistakes were 7_____. There were some 8_____ flaws, though, and the whole story was not very 9_____.

Wendy was very glad to get off the plane. She gave her grandparents a big hug. "Guess where we're taking you!" they announced. "We're going to Plymouth Rock to show you our 10_____ history."

"Great!" thought Wendy. "More travel—back in time again!"

Suffix Hopscotch

LOOK AT the root words in each hopscotch board. FILL IN the matching suffix at the top of the board.

HINT: Sometimes you have to drop or change a letter when you add a suffix.

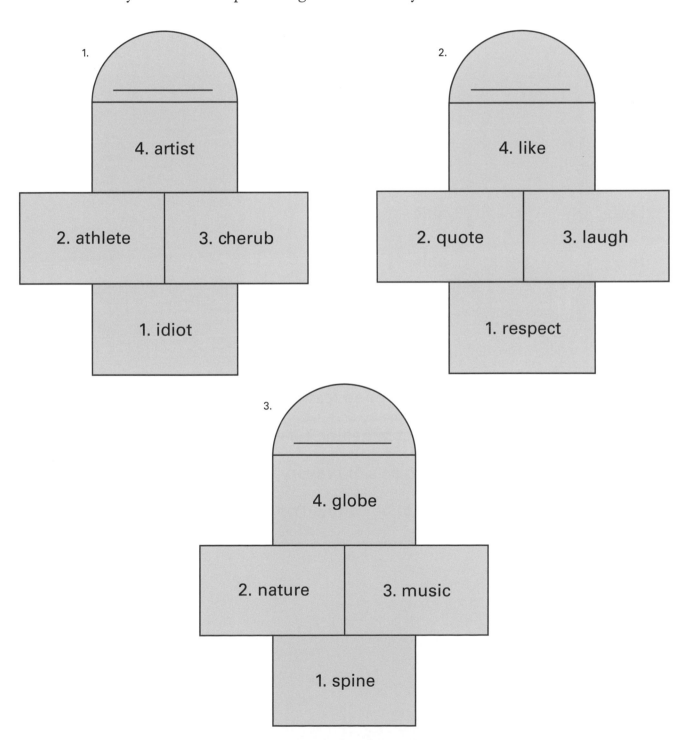

1.

4. artist

2. athlete   3. cherub

1. idiot

2.

4. like

2. quote   3. laugh

1. respect

3.

4. globe

2. nature   3. music

1. spine

Match Up

MATCH each root to a suffix. Then WRITE the word next to its definition.

Suffix Meanings: *-able, -ible = is able to   -al, -ial, -ic = relating to*

Root	Suffix
office	-ic
chew	-ial
dispose	-able
hero	-able
rely	-able

	Word	Definition
1.	_____	having formal authority
2.	_____	can use one's teeth to eat
3.	_____	the act of getting rid of something
4.	_____	doing acts of bravery
5.	_____	able to be counted on

Criss Cross

FILL IN the grid by answering the clues with keywords.

ACROSS

1. American period beginning in the 1600s
6. Can be worn inside-out
7. Not silent
8. Making sense
9. Seems possible

DOWN

1. Being relaxed with a pillow and blanket
2. Can be easily seen
3. Having lovely and flowing language
4. A play filled with songs
5. Something made of metal

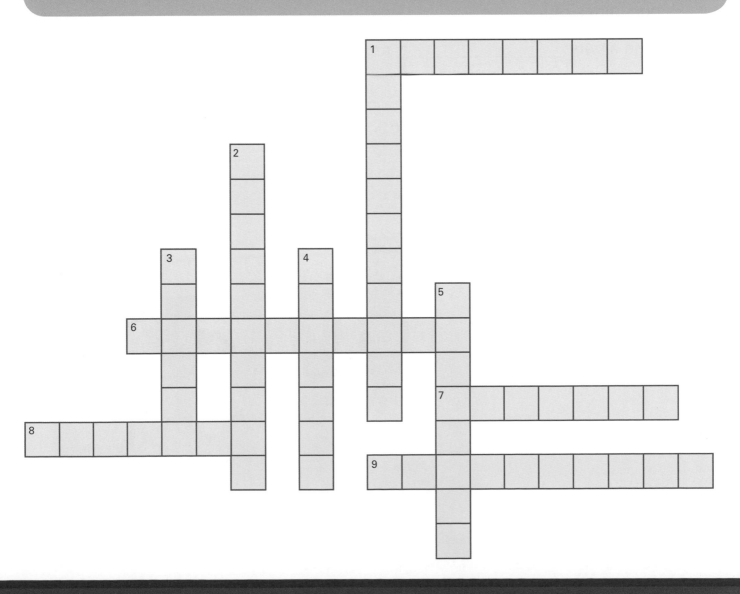

Blank Out!

FILL IN the blanks with keywords.

1. George played his music so loudly that it was _____ down the street.

2. Her new haircut was so _____ that everyone commented on it.

3. I can't carry a tune, but my brother is very _____.

4. Please make yourself _____ while you wait for me.

5. The excuse Susie gave her dad after coming home late wasn't very

    _____.

6. I like both sides of my _____ coat.

7. Lily made a very _____ argument to get her mom to let her go to the

    party.

8. Ruth's family took a trip to Williamsburg, Virginia to see _____ life in

    action.

9. Shakespeare's writing is very _____.

10. We hung _____

    decorations for the disco party.

Chopping Block

READ the words. CHOP OFF the suffix in each word by drawing a line right before the ending.
WRITE the root word in the blank.

HINT: You may have to add a letter or two to make the root word.

1. mistakable _____

2. sensible _____

3. historic _____

4. melodic _____

5. optical _____

6. teachable _____

7. robotic _____

8. volcanic _____

9. removal _____

10. valuable _____

Blank Out!

FILL IN the blanks with keywords.

1. An argument that makes sense is _____.

2. Someone who can play many instruments is _____.

3. European settlers who came to America in the 1600s had to adjust to

   _____ life in their new land.

4. Something that isn't silent is _____.

5. Something that can be worn inside-out is _____.

6. Something that rhymes is _____.

7. Something you can observe is _____.

8. Magnets will only stick to _____ surfaces.

9. When you're in a big easy chair by a fire, you feel _____.

10. A realistic story is _____.

Prefix Mix & Match

Think you've got your prefixes straight? It's time to check your skills. LOOK AT the prefixes and root words. WRITE all the words you can make by adding the prefixes to the roots.

anti-	im-	inter-	multi-	tri-
bi-	in-	mis-	trans-	uni-

cycle	centennial	biotic	pod
annual	match	national	perfect
continental	exact	focal	verse

_____

_____

_____

_____

_____

_____

_____

_____

_____

_____

_____

_____

_____

_____

_____

 **Check It!**

Page 191

Prefix Mix & Match

antibiotic
bicycle
biannual
bicentennial
bifocal
bipod
imperfect
inexact
intercontinental
international
inverse
mismatch
multinational
transcontinental
transverse
triannual
tricentennial
tricycle
trifocal
tripod
unicycle
universe

Page 192

Suffix Mix & Match

allergic, arrival, collectible, collection, collective, combinable, combination, completion, correctible, correction, corrective, divisible, division, divisive, erasable, historic, historical, imaginable, imagination, imaginative, locatable, location, lovable, loyalty, magical, mistakable, partial, partition, removable, removal, scenic, spatial, starvation, technicality, washable

Check It!

Page 193

Pathfinder

selection, mismatch, confusion, transplant, invention

Page 194

Sniglets!

1. antiloner
2. unisocks
3. translunch
4. ingymable
5. trimessaging

Suffix Mix & Match

Now it's time to test your knowledge of suffixes. LOOK AT the suffixes and root words. WRITE all the words you can make by adding the suffixes to the roots.

-able	-ative	-ic	-itive	-sion
-al	-ial	-ion	-ity	-sive
-ation	-ible	-ition	-ive	-ty

allergy	correct	locate	part	technical
arrive	divide	love	remove	wash
collect	erase	loyal	scene	
combine	history	magic	space	
complete	imagine	mistake	starve	

_____

_____

_____

_____

_____

_____

_____

_____

_____

_____

_____

Pathfinder

Think you know your prefixes and suffixes pretty well? Then you'll have no problem with this game. Begin at START. When you get to a box with two arrows, pick the prefix or suffix you can add to the root word. Then follow the prefix or suffix to the next root word. If you make all the right choices, you'll end up at FINISH.

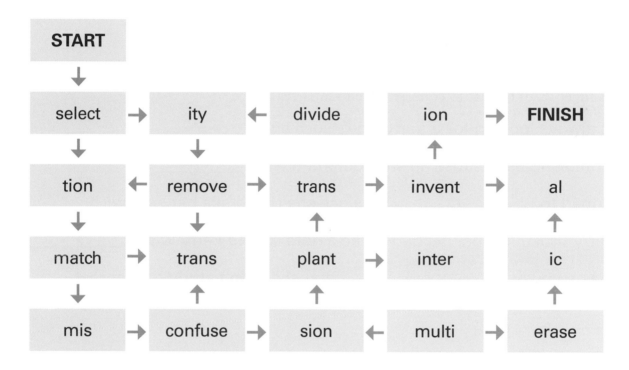

Sniglets!

Are you ready for some more sniglet fun? Remember, sniglets are fun-sounding words that haven't made it to the dictionary yet. Here are some sniglets made with the prefixes and suffixes you just reviewed.

unisocks—single, mismatched socks in your laundry basket

translunch—to swap lunches with a friend

trimessaging—emailing, texting, and IMing at the same time

antiloner—someone who does not like to be alone

ingymable—unable to participate in gym

WRITE a sniglet from the list to complete each sentence.

1. Dave is always looking for a party—he's such an _____.

2. Kylie wore sandals because all she could find were _____.

3. Mary hoped to _____ since she didn't like her sandwich.

4. After Perry broke his toe, his dad wrote a note saying Perry was _____.

5. Willa was so busy _____ that she didn't study for her test.

BONUS!

Now it's your turn. Here are some prefixes and suffixes you can use to create more sniglets.

magni- = large	tele- = distant
pro- = favor, for	co- = together

-arium = place for	-holic = addict
-cule = small	-ulent = full of

WRITE DOWN your sniglets and their definitions.

_____

_____

_____

_____

_____

Keywords

air•port—EHR-port *noun* level area where aircraft can take off and land

hab•it—HAB-iht *noun* something done often, by routine

hab•i•tat—HAB-ih-TAT *noun* an environment for human beings or other living things

ha•bit•u•al—huh-BIHCH-oo-uhl *adjective* done by habit

in•hab•it—ihn-HAB-iht *verb* to live somewhere

por•ta•ble—POR-tuh-buhl *adjective* able to be carried

por•ter—POR-ter *noun* someone who carries baggage

re•port—rih-PORT *noun* a detailed statement, paper, or account about a topic

sup•port—suh-PORT *verb* to hold something or bear weight

trans•port—tranz-PORT *verb* to take from one place to another

 Check It!

Page 196
Read & Replace
1. porter
2. portable
3. habit
4. habitual
5. transport
6. airport
7. report
8. inhabit
9. support
10. habitat

Page 197
Root It Out!
1. porter
2. support
3. habit
4. inhabit
5. habitat
6. transport
7. habitual
8. portable
9. report
10. airport

Page 198
Stack Up
HAB
1. rehabilitate
2. cohabit
3. uninhabited
4. haberdashery

PORT
1. import
2. important
3. export
4. deport

Page 199
Criss Cross

ACROSS	DOWN
4. habitat	1. habit
7. portable	2. habitual
8. support	3. inhabit
10. transport	5 airport
	6. report
	9. porter

Roots

Check It!

Read & Replace

ROOTS are groups of letters that can be found at the beginning, middle, or end of a word. Each root has its own meaning:

The root *hab* in the middle of the word *inhabit* means *hold* or *live*.
The root *port* at the end of the word *transport* means *carry*.

READ the story. FILL IN the blanks with keywords.

Their vacation was over. Mia's family had their bags packed. Her mother's suitcase was so big the 1_____ had to carry it to the lobby. "Do you have a 2_____ washing machine in there?" her father teased. Their mom had a 3_____ of overpacking, and her dad was a 4_____ jokester. A van came to 5_____ them to the 6_____. Mia noticed dark clouds in the sky. Her brother, Jack, launched into his annoying newscaster voice "Special 7_____. Hurricane warning. Expect travel to be disrupted." Mia rolled her eyes.

When the family arrived at the terminal, the building was packed. Flights were being cancelled. "It's getting serious, folks. Passengers may have to 8_____ the building." Jack announced. Many were sleeping on their luggage.

Mia sat down on the floor and leaned against a column for 9_____. "It's going to be a long evening," she sighed. "I guess I'll study the 10_____ of Gate 36!"

Root It Out!

READ each definition. WRITE the missing root letters in the blanks.

hab = have, hold, or live   port = carry

HINT: The **bold words** give you a clue about the root.

1. someone who **carries** your bags   ___ ___ ___ ___ er

2. **carry** weight   sup___ ___ ___ ___

3. a pattern of behavior that you **have**   ___ ___ ___ it

4. to **live** in a place   in___ ___ ___it

5. the environment where someone **lives**   ___ ___ ___itat

6. to **carry** something from one place to another   trans___ ___ ___ ___

7. **having** a repeated pattern of activity   ___ ___ ___itual

8. can be **carried**   ___ ___ ___ ___able

9. a paper that **carries** lots of information   re___ ___ ___ ___

10. a place with planes that **carry** people to faraway places   air___ ___ ___ ___

Stack Up

FILL IN a root in each word. WRITE the word in the column with that root. LOOK UP the definition. Can you see how it's related to its root?

re_____ilitate

im_____

co_____it

im_____ant

ex_____

de_____

unin_____ited

_____erdashery

HAB	PORT
have, hold, live	*carry*

1. _____   1. _____

2. _____   2. _____

3. _____   3. _____

4. _____   4. _____

Criss Cross

FILL IN the grid by answering the clues with keywords.

ACROSS

4. To help animals thrive, we must protect their ___.
7. You can take a laptop with you because it is ___.
8. Something to lean on
10. The subway can ___ passengers.

DOWN

1. Picking your nose is a bad ___.
2. Something you frequently do is ___.
3. Aliens might do this to Mars
5. Leave plenty of time to check in here
6. A kind of card with letter grades on it
9. Someone who will get your bags

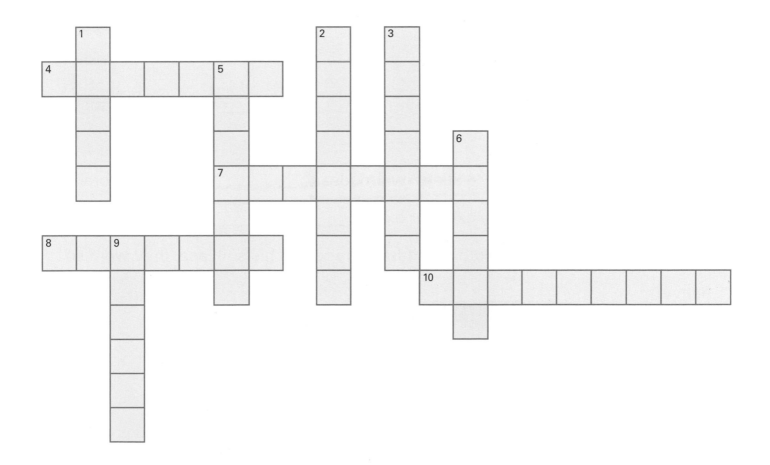

Roots

Blank Out!

FILL IN the blanks with keywords.

1. Lenny brought a _____ stove on the camping trip.

2. Zoey had a gross _____ of chewing her nails and spitting them out the window on car trips.

3. When they left town, the Coopers took a taxi to the _____.

4. Max says his brother belongs in a rainforest _____ with other monkeys.

5. My neighbor drives me crazy with his _____ 6 a.m. leaf-blowing and lawn mowing!

6. My sister had to use a wagon to _____ all her stuffed animals to the park.

7. After the concert, Nellie gave a glowing _____ to her friend about the new band.

8. My little brother's like a space alien—weird ideas _____ his brain.

9. Henry's grandmother uses a cane for extra _____.

10. The _____ asked Tom if he had rocks in his suitcase, they were so heavy!

It's Puzzling!

MATCH a prefix, root, and suffix to form a word. WRITE the words in the blanks.

 co-

 port

-it

_____

_____

_____

 im-

 hab

-ilitate

 re-

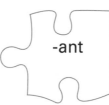 hab

-ant

Roots

Blank Out!

FILL IN the blanks with keywords.

1. This word tells how you get something to another place.

   You _____ it.

2. My sister turned to me for this when she argued with our parents to stay up late.

   _____

3. This word tells where you might go to pick up a visitor. _____

4. This word is what a hollowed out tree might be, for an owl. _____

5. Jay wears the same grubby grey sneakers every day because he's this kind of

   person. _____

6. This word tells what you might file with the police if your bike was stolen.

   _____

7. Cracking your knuckles is one example of this. _____

8. I felt like I had this job when Mom made me carry in all the groceries.

   _____

9. When you leave food on the counter, a colony of ants might do this to your kitchen.

   They might _____ it.

10. An inflatable mattress, a 10-inch
    TV, and a folding table all have
    this in common. They are
    all _____.

Keywords

ad•ver•tise—AD-ver-tiz *verb* to promote a product or service

at•tract—uh-TRAKT *verb* to pull something toward something else

con•trac•tion—kuhn-TRAK-shuhn *noun* the process of becoming smaller

con•vert•i•ble—kuhn-VER-tuh-buhl *adjective* able to change in form

dis•tract—dih-STRAKT *verb* to draw attention away from something

sub•tract—suhb-TRAKT *verb* to take away

trac•tion—TRAK-shuhn *noun* pulling power

trac•tor—TRAK-ter *noun* a large farm vehicle used to pull equipment

ver•ti•cal—VER-tih-kuhl *adjective* straight up and down

ver•ti•go—VER-tih-goh *noun* dizzying sensation of whirling motion

 **Check It!**

Page 204

Read & Replace

1. attract
2. convertible
3. subtract
4. advertise
5. tractor
6. traction
7. vertigo
8. distract
9. contraction

Page 205

Root It Out!

1. contraction
2. vertical
3. attract
4. convertible
5. advertise
6. distract
7. vertigo
8. tractor
9. subtract
10. traction

Page 206

Stack Up

VERT	TRACT
1. invert	1. retractable
2. vertebra	2. protract
3. extrovert	3. extract
4. introvert	4. detract

Page 207

Criss Cross

ACROSS	DOWN
1. vertical	2. contraction
5. attract	3. traction
8. vertigo	4. convertible
9. subtract	6. advertise
	7. distract

Read & Replace

 **Check It!**

Page 208

Blank Out!

1. convertible
2. traction
3. advertise
4. distract
5. vertigo
6. attract
7. subtract
8. tractor
9. contraction
10. vertical

Page 209

It's Puzzling!

diverted
extracted
extraction
extractable
introverted
reverted
retracted
retractable

Page 210

Blank Out!

1. vertigo
2. advertise
3. distract
4. vertical
5. attract
6. traction
7. contraction
8. convertible
9. tractor
10. subtract

The root *vert* at the beginning of the word *vertical* means *turn*, as in something turned on its end. The root *tract* at the end of the word *attract* means *pull*, as in two things pulled toward each other. Read the story. FILL IN the blanks with keywords.

advertise	attract	contraction	convertible	distract
subtract	traction	tractor	vertical	vertigo

Rosa and Samantha were waiting to order at the diner. Rosa picked up an ad for cars. "Which ones do you like?" she asked.

"The sporty ones 1_____ me. I like this cool red

2_____ car," said Samantha. "If I could only

3_____ a few thousand dollars from the price!"

"Hey, I guess farmers 4_____ in here," Rosa laughed.

"Check out this giant 5_____. It might work great in

the snow, with all that 6_____," she added.

"I don't know," said Samantha. "I think I'd get 7_____

climbing up that high." Just then the waitress came up. "I don't

mean to 8_____ you, young ladies," she said. "But

are you ready to order?"

"I'll have the 'VertiBurger'" said Rosa.

"What's that?" asked Samantha.

"It's our tallest burger," answered the waitress. "VertiBurger's

a 9_____ for Vertical Burger," she explained.

"Better not try one," said Rosa, "or you'll get dizzy!"

Root It Out!

READ each sentence. WRITE the missing root letters in the blanks.

> *vert = turn   tract = pull*

1. When you drop some letters and **pull** two words together, you form a

   con___ ___ ___ ___ ___ion.

2. When you **turn** something flat on its end, you make it ___ ___ ___ ___ical.

3. Bright lights always at___ ___ ___ ___ ___ tons of bugs.

4. You can **turn** a con___ ___ ___ ___ible sofa into a bed.

5. A new product can **turn** into a big hit if you ad___ ___ ___ ___ise it.

6. Having the television on can **pull** your attention away and dis___ ___ ___ ___ ___

   you from your book.

7. If the room seems to **turn** around and you feel dizzy, you may have

   ___ ___ ___ ___igo.

8. When a farmer needs to **pull** heavy farm equipment, he hitches it to his

   ___ ___ ___ ___ ___ or.

9. If you **pull** some money out of the bank, don't forget to sub___ ___ ___ ___ ___ it

   from your balance.

10. We tried to **pull** the sled up the hill but
    it was so slippery that it was hard to
    get ___ ___ ___ ___ ___ ion.

Stack Up

FILL IN a root in each word. WRITE the word in the column with that root.

LOOK UP the definition. Can you see how it's related to its root?

vert = turn   tract = pull

in_____

re_____able

pro_____

_____ebra

extro_____

intro_____

ex_____

de_____

VERT/VERS	TRACT
turn	*pull*

1. _____   1. _____

2. _____   2. _____

3. _____   3. _____

4. _____   4. _____

Criss Cross

FILL IN the grid by answering the clues with keywords.

ACROSS

1. Not horizontal

5. What magnets sometimes do to another

8. Head spinning feeling

9. Take away

DOWN

2. "Don't" instead of "do not"

3. What you get when you get a grip

4. Vehicle with a retracting roof

6. Promote

7. Take your mind off something

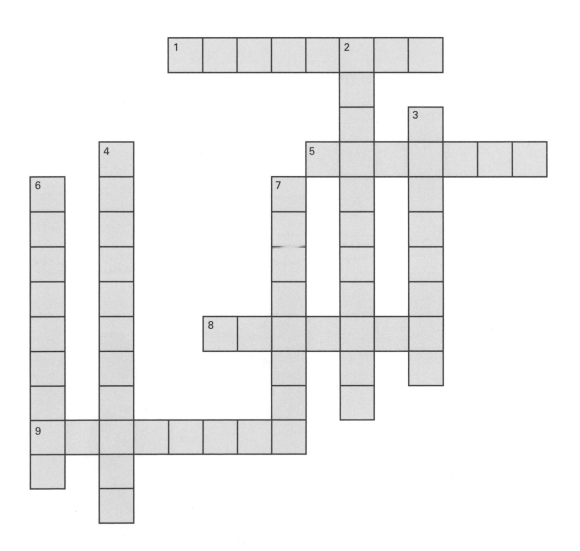

Blank Out!

FILL IN the blanks with keywords.

advertise	attract	contraction	convertible	distract
subtract	traction	tractor	vertical	vertigo

1. Sasha's toy was a _____ bulldozer that could turn into an army tank.

2. Ryan needed soccer cleats to get better _____ on the field.

3. If you want to get pet-sitting jobs, _____ in the local paper.

4. The cheerleaders tried to _____ the other team with their shouts and boos.

5. At the state fair, the ferris wheel gave Aunt Lin _____.

6. Jen thought her perfume would _____ boys, but it really smelled like dirty socks!

7. With this coupon, you can _____ $10 from your total purchase.

8. We hitched up the boat to a _____ to pull it to the lake.

9. Brad used a _____ to keep his text message as short as possible.

10. When I startled my cat, she did a crazy _____ leap.

It's Puzzling!

MATCH a prefix, root, and suffix to form a word. WRITE the words in the blanks.

HINT: You can use the same prefix, root, and suffix more than once.

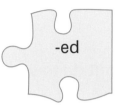     

re-   vert   -ed

_____

_____

_____

_____

di-   tract   -tion

_____

_____

_____

_____

ex-   -able

intro-

Blank Out!

FILL IN the blanks with keywords.

1. "Jerry is so tall. I'm surprised he doesn't get _____."

2. Barry's such a gossip. He likes to _____ my personal info to everyone we know.

3. This word tells what noise might do to you if you're trying to concentrate.

   _____

4. This word describes your position when you're standing up. _____

5. You might plant special bushes to do this to butterflies. _____

6. This word tells what you try to get when climbing up a slippery slope.

   _____

7. If you join two words together and drop a letter or two, you make this.

   _____

8. My sister thinks my bedroom is _____ and jumps and slides all over everything as if it was a playground too.

9. At the state fair, I saw people actually having this kind of race with their farm equipment. _____

10. This word tells what you need to do to turn 10 into 7.

    _____

Keywords

de•hy•drat•ed—dee-HI-dray-tuhd *adjective* having the water removed from

hy•drant—HI-druhnt *noun* a pipe for drawing water from a main pipe

hy•drate—HI-drayt *verb* to cause to absorb water

hy•dro•gen—HI-druh-jihn *adjective* a colorless gas that combines with oxygen to form water

hy•dro•pho•bi•a—HI-druh-FOH-bee-uh *noun* fear of water

ther•mal—THER-muhl *adjective* of or relating to heat

ther•mom•e•ter—ther-MAHM-ih-ter *noun* a device used for taking temperature

ther•mos—THER-muhs *noun* a container that keeps beverages hot or cold

ther•mo•stat—THER-muh-stat *noun* a device that regulates temperature

✓ Check It!

Page 212

Read & Replace

1. hydrant
2. Thermal
3. thermos
4. hydrate
5. thermometer
6. dehydrated
7. thermostat
8. hydrogen
9. hydrophobia

Page 213

Root It Out

1. dehydrated
2. hydrant
3. thermal
4. thermometer
5. thermostat
6. hydrophobia
7. hydrogen
8. thermos
9. hydrate

Page 214

Combo Mambo

THERM
1. thermonuclear
2. thermodynamics
3. thermoelectric

HYDR
1. hydroplane
2. hydraulic
3. hydroelectric

Page 215

Criss Cross

ACROSS
2. thermal
6. hydrogen
8. hydrant
9. thermostat

DOWN
1. thermos
3. hydrate
4. hydrophobia
5. thermometer
7. dehydrated

Read & Replace

Here are some more roots to add to your collection. The root *hydr* in the word *hydrate* means *water*. The root *therm* in the word *thermometer* means *heat*. READ the story. FILL IN the blanks with keywords.

Our camping trip was almost a disaster. It started out

smoothly enough. We met at the fire 1_____

near the corner to wait for the bus. Hallie, the leader,

asked us to check our backpacks. She called out a list.

2_____ underwear? Check! Flashlight? Check!

3_____ bottle? Check! Hallie reminded us it's

important to 4_____ ourselves on our hikes.

"The 5_____ showed the temperature was off

the charts today," she warned. "It's going to be a scorcher."

We took a long hike up a steep hill. We were all huffing and

puffing with our packs on our backs. Suddenly I noticed my

friend Liz didn't look good... and then she fainted. It turns

out she was 6_____. Hallie told us her body's

7_____ had overheated. Thankfully she recovered

when we gave her some H_2O (that's two molecules of

8_____ + oxygen = water!)

After that, we were glad to get to the campsite. Everyone was

eager to take a swim in the lake. Except Anna, that is. She was

shaking like a leaf. It turns out she has 9_____ and

was afraid to get anywhere near the lake!

Check It!

Page 216

Blank Out!

1. hydrate
2. hydrophobia
3. dehydrated
4. thermal
5. thermos
6. hydrant
7. thermostat
8. hydrogen
9. thermometer

Page 217

It's Puzzling!

dehydrate
dehydration
geothermal
rehydrate
rehydration

Page 218

Blank Out!

1. hydrant
2. dehydrated
3. thermostat
4. hydrophobia
5. thermal
6. hydrate
7. thermos
8. thermometer
9. hydrogen

Root It Out

READ the sentences. WRITE the missing root letters in the blanks to complete each keyword.

1. When you lose too much **water** you get de___ ___ ___ ___ated.

2. When a firefighter needs to hook his hose up to a **water** source, he looks for a ___ ___ ___ ___ant.

3. If you decide to go sledding, you'll want to stay conserve your **heat** with ___ ___ ___ ___ ___al leggings.

4. When you want to measure the **heat** outside, you look at the ___ ___ ___ ___ ___ometer.

5. When it gets really cold, you turn the **heat** up on the ___ ___ ___ ___ ___ostat.

6. If a person is really scared of **water**, he has ___ ___ ___ ___ophobia.

7. One of the two elements that combine to make **water** is ___ ___ ___ ___ogen.

8. If you don't want your soup to lose **heat**, you can put it in a ___ ___ ___ ___ ___ os.

9. To help your seeds grow, ___ ___ ___ ___ate them.

Combo Mambo

MATCH a word ending in a blue box to a root in a green box to make a word. WRITE the word in the root word box. LOOK UP the definition. Can you see how the word is related to *heat* or *water*?

HINT: You can use a word ending more than once.

oplane	onuclear	aulic	odynamics	oelectric

THERM

_____

_____

_____

HYDR

_____

_____

_____

Criss Cross

FILL IN the grid by answering the clues with keywords.

ACROSS

2. This kind of blanket can keep you warm

6. The "H" in H$_2$O

8. Don't park near a fire _____.

9. Turn this down to save energy in the winter

DOWN

1. Something to keep hot cocoa warm

3. Give liquid to

4. Fear of water

5. Tool used to check your temperature

7. Dried up

Blank Out!

FILL IN the blanks with keywords.

1. Drink a lot of water to _____ yourself during the tennis match.

2. Paul overcame his _____ by taking swimming lessons.

3. The plants looked a little _____ when we got back from our trip.

4. Jake's new _____ gloves kept his hands warm during the snowball fight.

5. Mandy brought cold lemonade in a _____ to the picnic.

6. Toby's dog always makes a beeline for that fire _____.

7. My mom turns up the temperature on the _____, and my dad keeps turning it down!

8. Did you know that there's more _____ than any other element in the universe?

9. Our oven _____ broke, and the brownies burned so much that the smoke alarm went off.

It's Puzzling!

MATCH a prefix, root, and suffix to form a new word. WRITE the words in the blanks.

HINT: You can use the same prefix, root, and suffix more than once.

re-   therm   -ation   _____

_____

_____

de-   hydr   -al   _____

_____

geo-   -ate

Blank Out!

FILL IN the blanks with keywords.

1. A _____ has a water pipe coming out of the street.

2. Someone who's very, very thirsty is _____.

3. You use a _____ to turn up the heat in a room.

4. Peter has _____, so he refused to go the water park with us.

5. _____ underwear keeps you warm.

6. We handed out cups of water at the marathon to help _____ the runners.

7. You should put hot tea in a _____ to keep it warm.

8. Caleb watched the _____ like a hawk, hoping the rain would change to snow.

8. When _____ combines with oxygen, you get water.

Keywords

ad•e•quate—AD-ih-kwiht *adjective* enough to satisfy

con•duct—KAHN-duhkt *noun* the way a person acts

de•duc•tion—dih-DUHK-shuhn *noun* the act of subtracting something

e•qual•i•ty—ih-KWAHL-ih-tee *noun* the state of being the same

e•qua•tion—ih-KWAY-zhuhn *noun* a mathematical statement in which two sides are equal

e•qua•tor—ih-KWAY-ter *noun* an imaginary line drawn around the middle of the Earth

e•qui•dis•tant—EE-kwih-DIHS-tuhnt *adjective* equally distant

eq•ui•ta•ble—EHK-wih-tuh-buhl *adjective* even-handed or fair

in•tro•duce—ihn-truh-DOOS *verb* to make someone known to another person

pro•duce—pruh-DOOS *verb* to make something

✓ Check It!

Page 220
Read & Replace

1. introduce
2. produce
3. equator
4. equidistant
5. equation
6. adequate
7. deduction
8. equitable
9. conduct
10. equality

Page 221
Root It Out

1. equidistant
2. introduce
3. conduct
4. adequate
5. produce
6. equation
7. deduction
8. equator
9. equality
10. equitable

Page 222
Stack Up

EQU
1. equilibrium
2. equinox
3. equilateral

DUC/DUCT
1. aqueduct
2. reproduce
3. viaduct

Page 223
Criss Cross

ACROSS	DOWN
2. equation	1. introduce
3. produce	2. equality
7. equidistant	4. adequate
8. deduction	5. equator
	6. conduct

 **Check It!**

Page 224

Blank Out!

1. deduction
2. equitable
3. conduct
4. introduce
5. equality
6. equator
7. adequate
8. equidistant
9. produce
10. equation

Page 225

It's Puzzling!

conductive
induction
inequity
reproduction
reproductive
unequivocal

Page 226

Blank Out!

1. equator
2. deduction
3. equidistant
4. adequate
5. Equality
6. produce
7. equitable
8. conduct
9. introduce
10. equation

Read & Replace

The root *equ* in the word *equal* means *the same*. The root *duct* in the word *conduct* means *lead*. Read the story. FILL IN the blanks with keywords.

Yesterday, my family went to the planetarium. We saw a new 3-D movie about our galaxy. First, the museum director came out to 1_____ the film. He was very proud because he helped 2_____ it.

Then, the lights went out and suddenly stars and planets were swirling around us. "You are standing on the middle of Planet Earth, right on the 3_____," boomed a deep voice. "You are 4_____ from the North and South poles." For a moment, I felt lost in the galaxy. But then the booming voice started rattling off a long 5_____ about how to calculate the distance of different planets. I thought I was back in math class! Just the sight of the stars would have been 6_____ without all of the explanations.

"Will there be a quiz at the end?" I whispered to my sister.

"Yes, and you'll get an automatic 7_____ of 20 points for talking during the movie," she whispered back. "Then so will you," I pointed out, to be 8_____.

My parents shushed us. "You guys have terrible 9_____. If you want 10_____," my dad said, "you can *both* go wait in the car!"

Root It Out

READ each sentence. WRITE the missing root letters in the blanks.

duc, duct = lead   equ, equi, equa = even, just

1. If two things are an **equal** distance apart from something they are

    ___ ___ ___ ___distant.

2. I **led** my friend to meet my mother so that I could intro___ ___ ___e them.

3. When you **lead** by example you demonstrate good con___ ___ ___ ___.

4. If something is just okay but could be better, it is ad___ ___ ___ ___te.

5. The baseball coach tried to **lead** the team to pro___ ___ ___e more hits.

6. The numbers on both sides of the equals sign are **even** in

    an ___ ___ ___ ___tion.

7. "The clues **lead** me to one elementary de___ ___ ___ ___ion,"

    said Sherlock Holmes.

8. The ___ ___ ___ ___tor is an **even** distance from Earth's two poles.

9. People must receive **even**-handed treatment for true ___ ___ ___ ___lity.

10. The pieces of cake were so

    uneven that it's not

    ___ ___ ___ ___table that

    my brother got the bigger piece!

Stack Up

FILL IN a root in each word. WRITE the word in the column with that root. LOOK UP the definition. Can you see how it's related to its root?

duc, duct = lead   *equ, equi, equa = even, just*

_____librium

aque_____

_____nox

repro_____

_____lateral

via_____

EQU /EQUI/ EQUA	DUC/DUCT
same	*lead*
1. _____	1. _____
2. _____	2. _____
3. _____	3. _____

Criss Cross

FILL IN the grid by answering the clues with keywords.

ACROSS

2. 52 + 6 = 58

3. Make

7. Two objects equally far from a place

8. Something taken away

DOWN

1. Help two people meet each other

2. Fairness

4. Just enough

5. An invisible line around the middle of the globe

6. Behavior

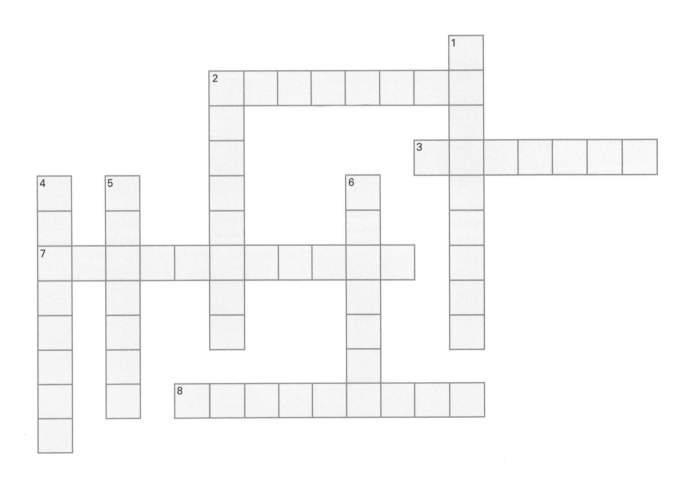

Blank Out!

FILL IN the blanks with keywords.

1. My parents paid for the game but said they'd make a _____ from my allowance.

2. After the job, the babysitters divided the payment in an _____ manner.

3. The police gave the hero who stopped the robber a medal for brave _____.

4. Lila worked up her nerve to _____ herself to the new boy on the block.

5. Civil rights leaders marched for _____ for all people.

6. The Earth is hottest near the _____.

7. Make sure to leave _____ room for dessert.

8. We tried to pick a meeting place that was _____ from our houses.

9. Maya's band hopes to _____ a CD when they have enough songs.

10. Lindsay had one more _____ to solve for her math homework.

It's Puzzling!

MATCH a prefix, root, and suffix to form a word. WRITE the words on the blanks.

HINT: You can use the same prefix, root, and suffix more than once.

repro-   equ   -ive

_____

_____

_____

in-   duct   -ity

_____

_____

_____

con-   -ivocal

un-   -ion

Blank Out!

FILL IN the blanks with keywords.

1. If you dislike hot weather, you would not want to live near the _____.

2. A _____ is a conclusion drawn from several observations.

3. The legs on my hemmed pants are not _____ from the floor. I look lopsided!

4. Something that's just good enough is _____.

5. _____ is when all people have the same rights.

6. Factory machines can _____ games quickly.

7. An even-handed solution is an _____ one.

8. Members of our Troop are bound by a code of good _____.

9. You might _____ to two friends who don't know each other at your birthday party

10. This word names a mathematical statement that contains an equals sign.

    _____

Pick the One!

You know your roots, right? So get going and check your skills! LOOK AT each group of words. Then CIRCLE the real word in each row.

Hint: Check to see if the words you find are in a dictionary!

1.	inhydrible	inhabitant	portity
2.	univert	supportive	habify
3.	tritractation	transvertate	rehabilitate
4.	thermoport	conducive	rehydrophobe
5.	irreversible	equality	antiduct
6.	mishabitate	importitude	introduction
7.	heliport	hydratical	revertical
8.	inthermia	equilibrium	transhabible
9.	retraction	misduce	multitherm
10.	intractial	misport	hydraulic

BONUS!

Pick a word from the list that is not a real word. Use what you know about prefixes, suffixes, and roots to write a definition. Use the "word" in a sentence.

_____

_____

_____

_____

✓ Check It!

Page 227

Pick the One!

1. inhabitant
2. supportive
3. rehabilitate
4. conducive
5. irreversible
6. introduction
7. heliport
8. equilibrium
9. retraction
10. hydraulic

Page 228

Match Up

Answers and suggested words:
1. c; hydrate, dehydrated, hydrogen
2. f; equation, equator, equality
3. h; habit, inhabit, habitual
4. g; thermal, thermos, thermometer
5. a; report, transport, portable
6. d; tractor, traction, distract
7. b; conduct, deduction, introduce
8. e; vertical, vertigo, advertise

Page 229

Pathfinder

import, introvert, distract, inhabit, extract

Page 230

Sniglets!

1. Inthermary
2. hydrovertation
3. ridicuport
4. habitipal
5. dustraction

Match Up

MATCH each root to its meaning. Then WRITE three words that contain each root.

Root		Meaning
1. hydr	_____	a. carry
2. equ	_____	b. lead
3. hab	_____	c. water
4. therm	_____	d. pull
5. port	_____	e. turn
6. tract	_____	f. even
7. duc	_____	g. heat
8. vert	_____	h. have/hold/live

1. _____

2. _____

3. _____

4. _____

5. _____

6. _____

7. _____

8. _____

Pathfinder

The game's the same, only the roots change. Begin at START. When you get to a box with two arrows, pick the root that you can add to the prefix. Then follow the prefix or suffix to the next root word. If you make all the right choices, you'll end up at FINISH.

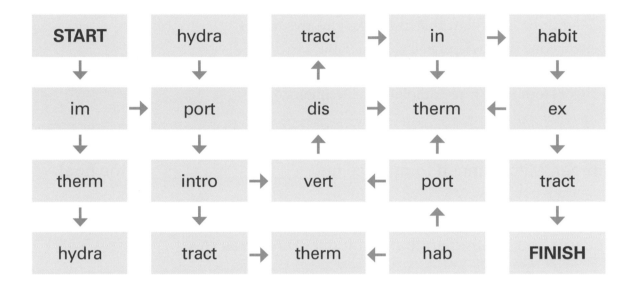

Sniglets!

Here are some sniglets made with the roots you just reviewed.

ridicuport—having far too much stuff to carry
hydrovertation—the ability to do somersaults in the water
inthermary—a place where overheated people go to cool off
dustraction—dust balls and lint that cling like glue to surfaces
habitipal—someone with whom you share a habit

WRITE a sniglet from the list to complete each sentence.

1. On scorching hot summer days, we call Josh's pool "The _____."

2. This summer, Milo planned to practice his _____ at the pool.

3. Kerry's backpack had so many books it was _____.

4. When it came to shooting spitballs at lunch, Dave was my _____.

5. After sleeping under the couch, our cat Fluffy was a walking lint ball, covered with

   _____!

Now it's your turn. Here are some roots you can use to create more sniglets. Use what you know about prefixes, suffixes, and roots to write a definition for each. The sillier the better!

cap = head (as in captain)	rupt = break (as in rupture)
mit = sent (as in transmit)	val = strong (as in value)
reg = rule (as in regulation)	

_____

_____

_____

_____

ad•dress¹—uh-DREHS *verb* 1. to speak about an issue 2. to deal with

ad•dress²—A-drehs *noun* information that gives the location of someone's home or business or e-mail account

ad•e•quate—AD-ih-kwiht *adjective* enough to satisfy

ad•ver•tise—AD-ver-tiz *verb* to promote a product or service

air•port—EHR-port *noun* level area where aircraft can take off and land

al•lowed—uh-LOWD *verb (past tense)* permitted

a•loud—uh-LOWD *adverb* 1. using the voice 2. not silently

a•muse—uh-MYOOZ *verb* 1. to charm or entertain 2. to make smile or laugh. Synonyms: charm, entertain, delight. Antonyms: bore, tire.

an•ti•bac•te•ri•al—AN-tee-bak-TEER-ee-uhl *adjective* active in killing germs

an•ti•slav•er•y—AN-tee-SLAY-vuh-ree *adjective* against the practice of owning people

an•ti•so•cial—AN-tee-SOH-shuhl *adjective* not wanting to be with other people

at•tract—uh-TRAKT *verb* to pull something toward something else

au•di•ble—AW-duh-buhl *adjective* able to be heard

be•liev•a•ble—bih-LEE-vuh-buhl *adjective* can be considered true

bi•an•nu •al—bi-AN-yoo-uhl *adjective* occurring twice a year

bi•cy•cle—BI-sihk-uhl *noun* a two-wheeled vehicle

bin•oc•u•lars—buh-NAHK-yuh-lerz *noun* a magnifying device with two lenses for seeing faraway objects

bud•dy—BUH-dee *noun* friend. Synonyms: pal, friend, chum. Antonyms: enemy, foe.

cer•tain•ty—SER-tuhn-tee *noun* the state of being sure

co•lo•ni•al—kuh-LOH-nee-uhl *adjective* referring to the 13 British colonies that became the United States of America

com•fort•a•ble—KUHM-fer-tuh-buhl *adjective* a state of well-being or ease

con•duct—KAHN-duhkt *noun* the way a person acts

con•struc•tion—kuhn-STRUHK-shuhn *noun* the process of building

con•trac•tion—kuhn-TRAK-shuhn *noun* the process of becoming smaller

con•vert•i•ble—kuhn-VER-tuh-buhl *adjective* able to change in form

creak—kreek *verb* to make a squeaking sound

cre•a•tive—kree-AY-tihv *adjective* capable of making or imagining new things

creek—kreek *noun* a small stream

de•ci•sive—dih-SI-sihv *adjective* having the power to make firm decisions

de•duc•tion—dih-DUHK-shuhn *noun* the act of subtracting something

de•hy•drat•ed—dee-HI-dray-tuhd *adjective* having the water removed from

dis•con•tin•ue—DIS-kuhn-TIHN-yoo *verb* to stop doing something. Synonyms: stop, end, terminate. Antonyms: continue, proceed, persist.

dis•tract—dih-STRAKT *verb* to draw attention away from something

ed•u•ca•tion—EH-juh-KAY-shuhn *noun* the act of learning or teaching

en•a•ble—ehn-AY-buhl *verb* to make possible. Synonyms: allow, permit, let. Antonyms: prevent, stop, prohibit.

e•qual•i•ty—ih-KWAHL-ih-tee *noun* the state of being the same

e•qua•tion—ih-KWAY-zhuhn *noun* a mathematical statement in which two sides are equal

e•qua•tor—ih-KWAY-ter *noun* an imaginary line drawn around the middle of the Earth

e•qui•dis•tant—EE-kwih-DIHS-tuhnt *adjective* equally distant

Vocabulary Words Index

eq•ui•ta•ble—EHK-wih-tuh-buhl *adjective* even-handed or fair

ex•cuse[1]—ihk-SKYOOS *noun* an explanation given to obtain forgiveness

ex•cuse[2]—ihk-SKYOOZ *verb* to overlook or forgive

ex•plo•sion—ihk-SPLOH-zhuhn *noun* a sudden burst, often loud or violent

hab•it—HAB-iht *noun* something done often, by routine

hab•i•tat—HAB-ih-TAT *noun* an environment for human beings or other living things

ha•bit•u•al—huh-BIHCH-oo-uhl *adjective* done by habit

hour—owr *noun* 1. a unit of time equaling 60 minutes 2. the time of day

hy•drant—HI-druhnt *noun* a pipe for drawing water from a main pipe

hy•drate—HI-drayt *verb* to cause to absorb water

hy•dro•gen—HI-druh-jihn *adjective* a colorless gas that combines with oxygen to form water

hy•dro•pho•bi•a—HI-druh-FOH-bee-uh *noun* fear of water

i•mag•i•na•tion—ih-MAJ-uh-NAY-shuhn *noun* the ability of the mind to create

im•mense—ih-MEHNS *adjective* very large. Synonyms: huge, vast, massive. Antonyms: tiny, minute, small.

im•po•lite—IHM-puh-LIT *adjective* 1. rude 2. lacking good manners

im•pos•si•ble—ihm-PAHS-uh-buhl *adjective* not able to occur

in•com•plete—ihn-kuhm-PLEET *adjective* not having all the necessary parts

in•cor•rect—ihn-kuh-REHKT *adjective* not having the right information

in•for•ma•tion—IHN-fer-MAY-shuhn *noun* facts or knowledge gained from any source

in•hab•it—ihn-HAB-iht *verb* to live somewhere

in•tel•li•gent—ihn-TEHL-uh-juhnt *adjective* smart. Synonyms: smart, bright, clever. Antonyms: stupid, ignorant, dense.

in•ter•na•tion•al—IHN-ter-NASH-uh-nuhl *adjective* between two or more countries

in•ter•sect—IHN-ter-SEHKT *verb* 1. to divide something by going across it 2. to cross or overlap

in•ter•state—IHN-ter-stayt *adjective* between two or more states

in•tro•duce—ihn-truh-DOOS *verb* to make someone known to another person

log•i•cal—LAHJ-ih-kuhl *adjective* resulting from clear thinking

me•tal•lic—muh-TAL-ihk *adjective* made of or containing metal

mis•be•have—MIHS-bih-HAYV *verb* to fail to act properly

mis•treat—mihs-TREET *verb* to deal with someone unfairly or cruelly

mis•un•der•stand—MIHS-uhn-der-STAND *verb* to fail to interpret something correctly

mul•ti•col•ored—MUHL-tih-KUHL-erd *adjective* having many hues

mul•ti•cul•tur•al—MUHL-tee-KUHL-cher-uhl *adjective* reflecting many different customs and backgrounds

mul•ti•mil•lion•aire—MUHL-tee-MIHL-yuh-NEHR *noun* someone a person who has millions of dollars

mul•ti•pur•pose—MUHL-tee-PER-puhs *adjective* having more than one use

mu•si•cal—MYOO-zih-kuhl *adjective* having a natural ability to carry a tune or play an instrument

no•tice•a•ble—NOH-tih-suh-buhl *adjective* can be easily observed

our—owr *pronoun* belonging to us

per•mis•sion—per-MIH-shuhn *noun* the act of allowing

plunge—pluhnj *verb* 1. to move abruptly forward or downward 2. to thrust into. Synonyms: dive, plummet. Antonyms: leap, climb.

po•et•ic—poh-EHT-ihk *adjective* 1. having a rhyming or lyrical quality 2. pleasing to the ear

po•lite—puh-LIT *adjective* showing good manners. Synonyms: respectful, courteous. Antonyms: rude, impolite, offensive.

por•ta•ble—POR-tuh-buhl *adjective* able to be carried

por•ter—POR-ter *noun* someone who carries baggage

prin•ci•pal—PRIHN-suh-puhl *noun* 1. the head of a school 2. the main leader of an activity or group

prin•ci•ple—PRIHN-suh-puhl *noun* a belief or value that helps guide behavior

prob•a•bly—PRAHB-uh-blee *adverb* very likely. Synonyms: likely, doubtless. Antonyms: unlikely, doubtfully.

pro•duce—pruh-DOOS *verb* to make something

proj•ect[1]—PRAH-jehkt *noun* a task

proj•ect[2]—pruh-JEHKT *verb* 1. to forecast 2. to jut out 3. to say loudly

re•cord[1]—REHK-erd *noun* 1. something official that preserves knowledge or history 2. best performance or greatest achievement

re•cord[2]—ri-KORD *verb* to make an audio, video, or written account of something

re•lax—rih-LAKS *verb* 1. to loosen up 2. to make less strict. Synonyms: unwind, loosen up, calm down. Antonyms: tense up, stiffen, strain.

re•port—rih-PORT *noun* a detailed statement, paper, or account about a topic

re•vers•i•ble—rih-VER-suh-buhl *adjective* 1. able to be turned back 2. can be worn inside out

sighs—siz *verb* breathes out audibly *noun* the sounds of sighing

sim•i•lar•i•ty—SIHM-uh-LAR-ih-tee *noun* the state of having a lot in common

size—siz *noun* 1. how big something is 2. the physical dimensions of an object

sub•tract—suhb-TRAKT *verb* to take away

sup•port—suh-PORT *verb* to hold something or bear weight

ther•mal—THER-muhl *adjective* of or relating to heat

ther•mom•e•ter—ther-MAHM-ih-ter *noun* a device used for taking temperature

ther•mos—THER-muhs *noun* a container that keeps beverages hot or cold

ther•mo•stat—THER-muh-stat *noun* a device that regulates temperature

trac•tion—TRAK-shuhn *noun* pulling power

trac•tor—TRAK-ter *noun* a large farm vehicle used to pull equipment

trans•con•ti•nen•tal—TRANZ-kahn-tuh-NEHN-tuhl *adjective* crossing a continent

trans•late—TRANZ-layt *verb* to convert one language to another

trans•port—tranz-PORT *verb* to take from one place to another

tri•an•gle—TRI-ang-guhl *noun* a shape with three sides

tri•ath•lon—tri-ATH-luhn *noun* a sports event with three different activities

trip•lets—TRIHP-lihts *noun* three children born at the same birth

tri•pod—TRI-pahd *noun* a three-legged stand

u•ni•corn—YOO-nih-korn *noun* an imaginary horse-like animal with a single horn

u•ni•cy•cle—YOO-nih-SI-kuhl *noun* a one-wheeled vehicle

u•ni•verse—YOO-nuh-vers *noun* all planets, space, matter, and energy in one whole

ver•ti•cal—VER-tih-kuhl *adjective* straight up and down

ver•ti•go—VER-tih-goh *noun* dizzying sensation of whirling motion

wound[1]—woond *noun* an injury

wound[2]—wownd *verb* 1. wrapped around something 2. changed direction

4th-Grade
Reading Comprehension
Success

When you're getting ready to read, you should think ahead. Ask yourself what you think you'll find out. Then, when you're done reading, look and see if what you read had all the answers to your questions.

Say you're going to read this article: "200 Years of Bicycles." Before you read, CHECK the box of each question you think this article will answer. (Don't try to answer the questions yet.) CROSS OUT the questions you don't think will be answered.

❏ 1. When were bicycles invented? _____

❏ 2. Who invented the wheel? _____

❏ 3. What was missing from the first bicycles?

_____

❏ 4. When was Susan B. Anthony born? _____

❏ 5. Why might bicycles replace cars? _____

_____

Now, READ the article.

200 Years of Bicycles

Bikes have come a long way since they were invented around 1818 in France. The first bicycles didn't even have pedals, you just pushed them along the ground with your feet! Now, almost 200 years later, we've got special bikes for roads, trails, and racing. Since bikes don't burn fuel or pollute the air, they may start to replace cars. Already, bicycles make up 40 percent of all traffic in the European city of Amsterdam. Even some American cities, like Portland, Oregon, are making cars give way to bikes on their streets. So start pedaling!

Go back and FILL IN the blanks in the questions you checked. Do you have all the answers? What about the questions you crossed out? Were you right?

✓ **Check It!**

Page 237

1. Around 1818.
2. X
3. Pedals.
4. X
5. They don't use fuel or cause pollution.

Page 238
Ask Questions!

1. 1895
2. X
3. 43
4. Asheville, North Carolina
5. X
6. Biltmore
7. 8000 acres
8. X
9. George Vanderbilt
10. X

Page 239
Ask Questions!

Suggestions:
-How long did it take to build?
-How much did it cost?
-What can you do for fun at Biltmore?
-What did Biltmore have that other homes of the time didn't have?

Page 240
Ask Questions!

1. Rocky Mountains
2. X
3. No
4. 150
5. X
6. 7–17
7. $3000 per session
8. X
9. Yes
10. Every night, weather permitting

 **Check It!**

Page 242

Ask Questions!

Suggestions:
-What can you do on Lake MacShane?
-What sports tournaments are there?
-What does "Kimimela" mean?
-Are boys allowed at Camp Kimimela?
-About how many campers are there?
-What are the cabins like?

Page 243

Ask Questions!

Possible Questions:
-What is the nose made out of?
-What is inside my nose?
-Why do we have snot?
-Why do we sneeze?
-How do we smell things?

Page 244

Ask Questions!

Did the article answer all of your questions?

Ask Questions!

Say you're going to read this article: "The Biggest Home in America."

Before you read, CHECK the box of each question you think this article will answer. CROSS OUT the questions you don't think will be answered.

☐ 1. When was the biggest home built?

_____

☐ 2. What is the capital of Kentucky?

_____

☐ 3. How many bathrooms does the biggest home have?

_____

☐ 4. Where is the biggest home in America?

_____

☐ 5. Did Ben Franklin really discover electricity?

_____

☐ 6. What is the biggest home called?

_____

☐ 7. How big is the backyard of the biggest home?

_____

☐ 8. Why can't penguins fly?

_____

☐ 9. Who built the biggest home?

_____

☐ 10. Is there a law that says kids can't stay up all night?

_____

Now, READ the article.

The Biggest Home in America

Would you like to live in the biggest home in America? Then head down to Asheville, North Carolina. That's where you'll find Biltmore—a palace built by millionaire George Vanderbilt in 1895. Don't forget to pack your swing set—Biltmore's backyard covers 8000 acres! And you'll need lots of toilet paper for the 43 bathrooms. There's also an indoor pool and bowling alley, just in case you get bored. The house took more than six years to build. No one's sure how much it cost, but consider this: it had electric lights, indoor bathrooms, central heating, and an elevator during a time when most people were still using outhouses and oil lamps!

Go back and FILL IN the blanks in the questions you checked. Do you have all the answers?

WRITE down three more questions that this article answers.

_____

_____

_____

_____

_____

Ask Questions!

Are you looking for a sleep-away camp? Read this brochure: "Be a Butterfly!"

Before you read, CHECK the box of each question you think this brochure will answer. CROSS OUT the questions you don't think will be answered.

❏ 1. Where is Camp Kimimela? _____

❏ 2. Are other camps better than Camp Kimimela? _____

❏ 3. Can I bring a cell phone to Camp Kimimela? _____

❏ 4. How many acres does Camp Kimimela cover? _____

❏ 5. Do lots of campers get homesick and leave Camp Kimimela? _____

❏ 6. How old are the campers? _____

❏ 7. How much does going to the camp cost? _____

❏ 8. How many kids have been injured at Camp Kimimela? _____

❏ 9. Can I play tennis and volleyball at Camp Kimimela? _____

❏ 10. When do they have campfires at Camp Kimimela? _____

Now, READ the brochure.

Be a Butterfly!

Camp Kimimela is a camp for girls in the beautiful Rocky Mountains. *Kimimela* means "butterfly" in the Native American Sioux language. Our campers stay in cabins named after different butterflies: Lacewings (ages 7–10), Swallowtails (ages 11–14), and Monarchs (15–17). While here, campers will live, play, and learn under the careful watch of a team of trained counselors.

Our camp is on 150 acres that include woods and a lake.

Camp activities include boating and swimming on beautiful Lake MacShane, as well as horseback riding and hiking in the woods. Campers may also join in sports tournaments (tennis, archery, and volleyball) and cabin skits and parties. Every day ends with a "Snack & Sing" around the campfire (weather permitting).

Our ten cozy cabins hold about 15 campers each. Don't worry—the cabins all have bunk beds, electricity, and bathrooms!

Since Camp Kimimela is all about outdoor fun, you may not bring cell phones, MP3 players, or hand-held game systems. Parent phone calls are limited to one per week.

Our six-week sessions run from June to mid-July and mid-July through August. The cost is $3000 per session for one child. The deadline for applications is May 1st.

If you have any questions, please contact our management office.

GO BACK and FILL IN the blanks in the questions you checked. Do you have all the answers?
WRITE down five more questions that this article answers.

_____

_____

_____

_____

_____

Ask Questions!

Curious about your sniffer? Read the article on the following page: "Your Nose: Inside and Out." Before you read, WRITE some questions you think this article will answer. There's extra room so you can come back after you read and fill in the answers.

1. Question: _____

_____

_____

_____

2. Question: _____

_____

_____

_____

3. Question: _____

_____

_____

_____

4. Question: _____

_____

_____

_____

Now, READ the article.

Your Nose: Inside and Out

Noses come in all shapes and sizes. The part that sticks out of your face isn't bone—it's mostly *cartilage*, a kind of tissue that is strong, but wobbly.

Men have longer noses than women, but women have a better sense of smell!

When we breathe through our noses, we suck in way more than just air. That's why we need hair and snot in our noses! Snot (also called *mucus*) is made out of water, salt, and other chemicals so it's thick and sticky. The hair blocks the dust, pollen, and other bad junk from getting into your lungs. Then the snot sticks to it and pulls it down into your stomach when you sniff and swallow. Or, you can blow the bad junk out of your nose, along with the snot.

A strong sneeze can shoot snot out of your nose at over 100 miles per hour!

What about smell? Odor molecules are very light, and they float up through your nose to the very back. That's where you've got a bunch of nerves that catch odors and report them to your brain.

Your sense of smell goes hand in hand with your sense of taste. If something smells rotten, you probably won't eat it because your nose knows it will make you sick! Thanks, Sniffie!

GO BACK and look at the questions you asked. ANSWER them. ADD any new questions and the answers you learned here.

_____

_____

_____

_____

✓ Check It!

Cut out the Check It! section on page 237, and see if you got the answers right.

Another question to ask yourself before reading is "What do I already know?" Then, when you're done reading, you can ask: "What did I learn?" Try it out!

First, READ the topic. Then FILL IN the What Do I Already Know? column. After that, you'll be ready to read!

Topic: Tomatoes

What Do I Already Know?

_____

_____

_____

_____

_____

_____

_____

What Did I Learn?

_____

_____

_____

_____

_____

_____

_____

There's Nothing Rotten about Tomatoes!

We all know that tomatoes are good for us. But did you know that tomatoes are actually fruit? That's right! Tomatoes contain seeds and grow from a flowering plant—just like a strawberry. But since the tomato isn't sweet, it's generally considered a vegetable. Here's another fact about tomatoes: Every August, a town in Spain hosts *La Tomatina*, a massive food fight using tons of rotten tomatoes. Sounds like fun—as long as you don't have to clean up afterward!

Time to GO BACK and FILL IN the What Did I Learn? column. CROSS OUT any facts in the first column you got wrong. See how this works?

✓ Check It!

Page 245

Suggestions:
Know:
1. Tomato is red.
2. Tomato is a veggie.
3. Tomato is good for you.
4. You make ketchup out of tomatoes.

Learned:
1. Tomatoes are fruit.
2. Fruits contain seeds and grow from flowering plants.
3. A town in Spain has a tomato fight every year.

Page 246

Suggestions:
Know:
1. There are nine planets.
2. The planets revolve around the sun.
3. Jupiter is the biggest planet.
4. Saturn has rings.

Learned:
1. Pluto is not a planet.
2. The sun is the largest object in the solar system.
3. The system also includes moons, comets, and asteroids.
4. There are three asteroids in close orbit to Earth.
5. There's an asteroid belt.

Page 248

Suggestions:
Know:
1. Spiders are bugs.
2. Spiders are deadly.
3. Spiders spin webs.
4. The tarantula is big and hairy.

Learned:
1. Spiders aren't insects.
2. Spiders are carnivores.
3. Few spiders actually hurt humans.
4. The tarantula can kill with its hair.
5. Some spiders hunt without webs.

✓ Check It!

Page 250

Suggestions:

Know:
1. Fairies aren't real.
2. I know about the tooth fairy.
3. Fairies have magic.
4. I've read about fairies in stories.

Learned:
1. There are lots of fairies in fiction.
2. People used to really believe in fairies.
3. *Brownies* and *pookahs* are kinds of fairies.
4. People used iron to ward off fairies.
5. There is a legend behind the tooth fairy.
6. Two girls took fake fairy photos in 1917.

Before & After Questions

FILL IN the What Do I Already Know? column.

Topic: The Solar System

What Do I Already Know?	What Did I Learn?
_____	_____
_____	_____
_____	_____
_____	_____
_____	_____
_____	_____
_____	_____
_____	_____
_____	_____
_____	_____
_____	_____
_____	_____
_____	_____
_____	_____
_____	_____
_____	_____
_____	_____

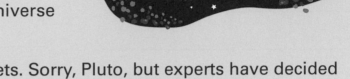

Now, READ the article.

Our Corner of the Universe

The solar system is nine planets and the sun, right? WRONG. There's a lot more going on in our little corner of the universe than you think.

First of all, there are only eight planets. Sorry, Pluto, but experts have decided that you're not really a planet. (That's okay, Earth still loves you!)

So the planets of the solar system are: Mercury (closest to the sun), then Venus, Earth, Mars, Jupiter, Saturn, and Neptune.

Pluto used to come last in the lineup. But now it's considered a *dwarf planet*, which means that it's not really big enough to count as a planet. Other dwarf planets are Ceres and Eris.

There's more to the solar system than just the planets. The sun, of course, is the largest object in the solar system. But the system also includes moons, comets, and asteroids.

Scientists have learned a lot about the biggest asteroids. There are three that have orbits close to Earth: Atens, Apollos, and Amors. There's also a huge *asteroid belt* between Mars and Jupiter. This "belt" is like a highway for lots of asteroids.

It may sound like the solar system is a crowded place. Not! There are millions (sometimes billions) of miles between the planets and asteroids. They don't call it "space" for nothing!

Did you learn anything? GO BACK and FILL IN the What Did I Learn? column.

Before & After Questions

FILL IN the What Do I Already Know? column.

Topic: Spiders

What Do I Already Know?

_____

_____

_____

_____

_____

_____

_____

_____

_____

_____

_____

_____

_____

_____

What Did I Learn?

_____

_____

_____

_____

_____

_____

_____

_____

_____

_____

_____

_____

_____

_____

Now, READ the article.

Tiny Hunters: Spiders

Spiders are really interesting creatures, but they're not insects. Nope! Spiders are arachnids. Unlike insects, arachnids have eight (or more) legs, and they don't have antennae or wings. Other famous arachnids include scorpions and ticks. Spiders are *carnivores*, which means that they eat other living creatures.

All spiders can spin webs. Some spiders use webs to catch insects. But other spiders actually hunt their prey, just like tiny lions. A large tarantula can chase down and kill a small lizard or a bird!

The tarantula is probably the scariest spider. It can grow as big as 4 inches, with 12-inch legs. But tarantulas hardly ever bite, and they're generally harmless. People even keep them as pets! Strange fact: Some tarantulas have sharp, poisonous body hair that they throw at attackers. The poison on these hairs can kill a small mouse.

Most spiders bite, though, and use poison to protect themselves or kill their prey. But very few kinds of spiders can hurt humans. In all of North America, there are only five or six really harmful kinds, including the black widow and the brown recluse. Still, any time you get a spider bite, you should get it checked out!

Did you learn anything? GO BACK and FILL IN the What Did I Learn? column.

Before & After Questions

FILL IN the What Do I Already Know? column.

Topic: Fairies

What Do I Already Know?

_____

_____

_____

_____

_____

_____

_____

_____

_____

_____

_____

_____

_____

What Did I Learn?

_____

_____

_____

_____

_____

_____

_____

_____

_____

_____

_____

_____

_____

Now, READ the article.

Fairies: Fact & Fiction

There are lots of famous fairies in fiction. Where would Cinderella be without her fairy godmother? Or Peter Pan without Tinkerbell? Narnia is filled with fairies! Even more recent books, like *Artemis Fowl* and the *Spiderwick Chronicles*, are about people who try to learn all the secrets of the fairy world.

For hundreds of years, many people really believed in fairies. They blamed fairies for strange weather, natural wonders, or sudden illness. They thought naughty fairies like *brownies* and *pookahs* would steal objects or damage crops. Some thought bad fairies would take human babies and replace them with fairy babies (called *changelings*). They even blamed fairies when they got lost in the woods!

To get rid of fairies, people used iron, four-leaf clovers, or even bread. But not everybody disliked fairies. People who wanted to attract fairies built little houses for them to live in!

TURN the page to keep reading!

The most famous fairy story is, of course, about the tooth fairy. In the old days, some people believed that baby teeth were really powerful. They thought if a mean fairy took the teeth, she could work evil magic on the children. So, parents would bury their kids' teeth to keep them safe. Later, this practice changed to "burying" the tooth under a pillow or in a glass of water by the bed. Then, people thought the tooth fairy (a good fairy) would come and replace the tooth with money or a gift. This is a much nicer legend!

In 1917, two young girls took photographs of fairies flying around their backyard in Cottingley, England. The photos looked so real that people believed they were proof that fairies existed. Even the author of the *Sherlock Holmes* books, Sir Arthur Conan Doyle, was a believer! Years later, one of the girls confessed that all the pictures were fakes. The "fairies" were really cut out of paper. But in 2001, their photos sold for over $12,000!

There will always be people who want to believe in fairies. How about you?

Did you learn anything? GO BACK and FILL IN the What Did I Learn? column.

Check It!

Cut out the Check It! section on page 245, and see if you got the answers right.

Sometimes authors are tricky. They like to write about things without actually telling you what those things are. Why? Because it makes you curious. It makes you read between the lines!

READ this story.

> **Timmy and the Truck**
>
> Timmy had lived at 328 Hampton Drive ever since he was little. It was an exciting place! Every now and then, a loud bell would ring, and all the men would drop what they were doing, slide down a pole, and jump on a big red truck. Then the truck would race out of the garage, lights blazing and siren screaming. Timmy wished he could ride the truck too. But he was always there when the truck came back, wagging his tail and barking "Hello!"

Now, CHECK the right answers, and FILL IN the blanks.

1. What's at 328 Hampton Drive?

   ☐ a. A dance club

   ☐ b. A Chinese restaurant

   ☐ c. A firehouse

   How do you know?

   _____

2. Who is Timmy?

   ☐ a. A fireman

   ☐ b. A little boy

   ☐ c. A fire dog

   How do you know?

   _____

See? You're too smart to let an author trick you. Let's do some more!

✓ **Check It!**

Page 253

1. c: fire bell, fire pole, big red truck
2. c: wags tail and barks

Page 254
Check, Please!

1. c: same mom, Ophelia is two minutes older
2. a: front seat, pedaling, "backseat biker"

Page 255
Check, Please!

1. a: kids are dancing, yummy food
2. c: Zella is Red Riding Hood, Evan's a clown, Tory's a vampire
3. b: people moo at Amit and ask him for milk

Pages 256-257
Check, Please!

1. c: face is pale, hands are shaking
2. b: corset, hoop skirts, President Lincoln
3. a: "joined up," fighting rebels, he's on Lincoln's side
4. c: Helena stepped out the front door then sat down.
5. b: work in her lap, wool, needles

Check It!

Pages 258-260

Author! Author!

Ask a friend to read your stories
to try to read between the lines!

Check, Please!

READ this story.

> **On the Go**
>
> "I want to ride in front!" yelled Ophelia.
> "Too bad," said Felix. "I got on first."
> "But I'm the oldest."
> "Only by, like, two minutes. Get over it and start pedaling!"
> "Where are we going?" asked Ophelia.
> "To see Mom at her office," said Felix.
> "That's like three miles! We'll never make it!"
> "You're out of shape."
> "Watch out! You almost hit that cat."
> "Stop being a backseat biker!"

Now, CHECK the right answers, and FILL IN the blanks.

1. Who are Ophelia and Felix?

☐ a. Best friends

☐ b. Worst enemies

☐ c. Twins

How do you know?

_____

2. What are they doing?

☐ a. Riding a bicycle built for two

☐ b. Driving a car

☐ c. Riding their bikes

How do you know?

_____

Check, Please!

READ this story.

Moo!

Everyone was having a great time, except for Amit. Sure, there was yummy food, and some kids were dancing, but Amit was mad. His friend Zella looked great in her red riding hood, and Evan made a funny-looking clown. This only made Amit madder.

"What's wrong, Amit?" asked Tory, who was a vampire. "Aren't you having fun?"

"If one more person moos at me, or asks if I 'got milk,' I'm leaving!"

Tory laughed. "Poor Amit! Maybe you should have worn something else."

Now, CHECK the right answers, and FILL IN the blanks.

1. **Where is Amit?**

   ☐ a. At a party   ☐ b. In school   ☐ c. Selling candy door-to-door

   How do you know?

   _____

2. **What kind of party is it?**

   ☐ a. A birthday party   ☐ b. A slumber party   ☐ c. A costume party

   How do you know?

   _____

3. **What is Amit wearing?**

   ☐ a. A space suit   ☐ b. A cow costume   ☐ c. A wizard's hat

   How do you know?

   _____

Check, Please!

READ this story.

Wally at War

It was a hot day, and Helena's corset was tight around her rib cage as she washed the dishes.

"Helena!" called Mama. "Come out here for a minute."

"Yes'm," Helena said. She stepped out the front door and dropped into a chair, arranging the hoops under her skirts so that they didn't stick up.

"Mr. Birdsley came by," said Mama. Her face was pale and her work was lying in her lap. "He says there's a big battle going on over in Gettysburg, Pennsylvania."

Helena gasped. "Pennsylvania! But that's where Wally's last letter came from! Do you think...?"

Mama's hands were shaking as she picked up a ball of wool that had fallen. "I told that boy not to join up and fight those rotten rebels!"

"He's trying to keep this country together, Mama," said Helena. "Mr. Lincoln says—"

"I don't care what the President says!" Mama snapped. Suddenly, she burst into tears, and her long needles fell to the floor with a clack.

Now, CHECK the right answers, and FILL IN the blanks.

1. Why is Mama crying?

☐ a. She's angry at Helena.

☐ b. She's angry at Wally.

☐ c. She's afraid for Wally.

How do you know?

_____

2. When does this scene take place?

☐ a. In the future

☐ b. In the past

☐ c. Present day

How do you know?

_____

3. Who is Wally?

☐ a. A soldier fighting in a war

☐ b. A farmer

☐ c. A newspaper reporter

How do you know?

_____

4. Where are Mama and Helena sitting?

☐ a. In the kitchen

☐ b. At church

☐ c. On the front porch

How do you know?

_____

5. What was Mama doing?

☐ a. Working on a crossword puzzle

☐ b. Knitting

☐ c. Shelling peas

How do you know?

_____

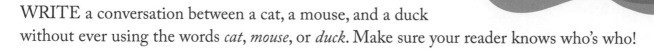

Author! Author!

Now it's YOUR turn!

WRITE a conversation between a cat, a mouse, and a duck
without ever using the words *cat*, *mouse*, or *duck*. Make sure your reader knows who's who!

HINT: How would a cat talk to a mouse? Would a duck have a funny voice? What would their names be? What do they look like?

Author! Author!

WRITE about an argument between best friends about their favorite TV shows. And get this: the kids are in a cave on a camping trip. But don't say they're in a cave, and don't use the words *TV* or *television*.

HINT: What are the names of the TV shows? What do the kids like about them? What do you find in caves? Bats? Stalactites? How would their voices sound in a cave?

_____

_____

_____

_____

_____

_____

_____

_____

_____

_____

_____

_____

_____

_____

_____

_____

_____

_____

_____

_____

_____

_____

Author! Author!

WRITE about a kid playing checkers with his dad on a sailboat in the ocean. Don't say that they're on a sailboat. Don't use the word *checkers*.

HINT: You can say "King me!" or "I'll be red." You can talk about the parts of the sailboat, or how it's rocking on the ocean. Describe the ocean too!

_____

_____

_____

_____

_____

_____

_____

_____

_____

_____

_____

_____

_____

_____

 **Check It!**

Cut out the Check It! section on page 253, and see if you got the answers right.

You know the difference between a fact and an opinion, right? Did you know that they work together? Yep! If you've got an opinion, you should back it up with some facts. Check it out:

Question: Should kids have cell phones?

FILL IN some more facts to support each opinion.

OPINION	FACTS
YES	Kids can call parents in an emergency.
YES	Home phone lines aren't tied up.
YES	Kids can be more independent.
YES	_____
YES	_____
YES	_____
NO	Kids will use the phone too much.
NO	Phones and minutes are expensive.
NO	Kids could lose the phone or have it stolen.
NO	_____
NO	_____
NO	_____

Any time a news story or nonfiction article states an opinion, you should always look for the facts. Then you can make up your OWN mind!

✓ Check It!

Page 261

Suggestions:
YES:
1. Phones are cool.
2. Kids need to learn to use this essential gadget.
3. Kids can learn about managing money from the monthly bill.

NO:
1. Phones keep kids from socializing in person.
2. Phones keep kids from playing outside or exercising.
3. Phones in school or at the dinner table are bad manners.

Page 263

Suggestions:
YES:
1. Skaters can teach each other tricks.
2. Skaters could have a tournament.
3. Pietown could become famous for skateboarding.

NO:
1. It's not safe for kids who don't skate well.
2. Skater kids may misbehave.
3. It'll cost $5 to get in.

Page 265

Suggestions:
YES:
1. Next-door neighbors.
2. Thalia comes when Sabeena needs her.
3. Thalia knows how to cheer Sabeena up.
4. Families are best friends too.

NO:
1. Thalia borrows stuff and doesn't give it back.
2. Thalia tells lies about Sabeena to other kids.
3. Thalia is a bad sport.
4. Thalia is a hair-puller.

Page 268

Fact & Opinion

Suggestions:
YES:
1. Zoos have been around since 1793.
2. Animals are cared for in zoos: fed, safe, and healthy.
3. Scientists and the public learn a lot from animals in zoos.
4. Families can't see many animals in the wild.
5. Zoos breed endangered animals.

Continued on the back

✓ Check It!

Page 268

Suggestions:
NO:
1. Animals aren't comfortable: there's no space.
2. Animals aren't behaving naturally in zoos.
3. Animals develop strange behaviors in zoos.
4. It's better to save the natural habitats of wild animals, because that helps the planet.
5. Only a few species have survived being born in captivity.

Q: Should Pieville open a skate park?

First, READ the news story.

New Skate Park on Mozzarella Street

Pietown is buzzing about Mayor Bixby Stiggle's plan to build a skate park next to the library.

"Pietown supports young athletes," said the mayor. "We provide basketball courts and baseball diamonds. A skate park is a logical next step."

"Why should those skater kids get a park? This town needs a good playground for toddlers first!" said Eva T. Finkle, who lives near the library.

Donald Sabin is pleased about the plan, but worried: "If it keeps skaters out of the empty pools in town, that's great. But is it safe for kids who don't skate well? And some of those skater kids are bad news. Will there be a grownup making sure everyone behaves?"

But his son DJ can't wait to try it out: "It'll be great to have a place just for skaters. It's a chance for us to get together and teach each other tricks. Maybe we can even have a tournament. Pietown could be famous for skateboarding!"

There is one thing that DJ doesn't like, though: The town will probably charge skaters $5 to enter the park.

Now, FILL IN the facts.

OPINION	FACTS
YES	The town builds other sports areas for kids, like baseball diamonds.
YES	It'll keep skaters out of the empty pools in town.
YES	_____
YES	_____
YES	_____
NO	Pietown needs a toddler playground first.
NO	It might not be safe for new skaters.
NO	_____
NO	_____
NO	_____

So? What do YOU think?

Should Pietown open a skatepark?

Circle one: YES   NO

Q: Should Sabeena stay best friends with Thalia?

First, READ Sabeena's diary.

Sabeena's Problem

Dear Diary:

I don't think I can be best friends with Thalia anymore. I mean, I know we've been friends since kindergarten, but people change. Like, we both used to love all the same things: Barbies, roller-skating, and playing pretend. But now, I'm really into soccer and ballet, while all Thalia can talk about is boys and computers.

On the other hand, it would be hard for us to stop being friends because we're next-door neighbors. I can just yell out the window when I want to hang out. Thalia always comes when you need her!

But she's a terrible friend! She borrows stuff and never gives it back—like my favorite hoodie. And she's definitely been telling lies about me behind my back at school.

When she's being nice, Thalia is so much fun. Nobody else knows how to cheer me up like she does. And our families are best friends too!

But still! The other day, when I beat her at volleyball, she pulled my hair. Who wants to be friends with a hair-puller?

Thanks for listening, Diary.

—Sabeena

Now, FILL IN the facts.

OPINION	FACTS
YES	They've been friends since kindergarten.
YES	_____
YES	_____
YES	_____
YES	_____
NO	They don't have the same interests anymore.
NO	_____
NO	_____
NO	_____
NO	_____

So? What do YOU think?

Should Sabeena stay best friends with Thalia?

Circle one: YES   NO

Fact & Opinion

Q: Should animals be kept in zoos?

First, READ the news story.

Concrete Jungle

People have been arguing about zoos ever since the first zoo opened to the public in 1793. It's a real knock-down, drag-out fight!

"Zoos are not comfortable for animals. In a zoo, birds have their wings clipped so they can't fly," says animal rights activist Mr. Leon Fribble. "And elephants, that often walk 20 to 30 miles a day, only have a little bit of space to move around."

Zookeepers don't agree. "Animals in zoos are fed every day, and they're safe from attack," says Mr. Hyram Higgins of the Pietown Zoo. "We even have doctors to take care of them when they're sick."

Plus, Higgins adds, "Not only do scientists learn a lot from animals in zoos, but ordinary people come every day to watch animals they would never normally see. It's a great lesson!"

But Fribble and other activists don't think that the chance for learning is worth keeping animals captive. "What are we learning?" Fribble asks. "These animals aren't living naturally. In the wild, their behavior is all about finding food. In zoos, they don't need to hunt, they don't need to make their own homes. They're not doing anything! Except maybe going a little crazy."

Fribble points out that animals living in small spaces, with humans constantly staring at them, can develop strange behaviors. For instance, animals might walk in the same circle all day long, or try to hurt themselves.

"Animals don't act like that in the wild. The only way you can learn about them is by watching them in their natural habitats," says Fribble.

But how many families can visit Africa to see a lion in the wild?

"We no longer live with many wild animals, like in the old days," says Higgins. "We've killed off most of the wolves and the bears and the buffalo. Zoos are our only chance to be near them."

The greatest benefit that zoos can give to animals is species preservation. Since the 1970s, zoos have worked hard to breed animals that are endangered. But their success has been limited. Only a few wild animals can survive being born and raised in captivity.

Some people think it would be better to preserve the animals' natural habitats.

"After all," says environmentalist Ms. Sindy Hoo, "if we save a jungle or a swamp, it's not just good for the animals that live there. It's good for the whole planet!"

Now, turn the page to FILL IN the facts.

Now, FILL IN the facts.

OPINION	FACTS
YES	_____
YES	_____
YES	_____
YES	_____
YES	_____
NO	_____
NO	_____
NO	_____
NO	_____
NO	_____

So? What do YOU think?

Should animals be kept in zoos?

Circle one: YES   NO

Check It!

Cut out the Check It! to see if you got the answers right.

Skimming

They say a picture's worth a thousand words. Especially if it's a graph, a chart, or a map. When you're skimming an article, don't forget to slap your eyes on the pictures. SKIM this article.

HINT: Notice anything funny about this page? We've already blurred the words you can skip.

Pizza Time in Pietown

Pizza's Popular Seven Days a Week

Riusting eqs euis auguer sed min laorger cilit, corsequ amconum a dio corsecten doloreet num deli te digna feum ex eu facnum in at Riusting eqs euis auguer sed min laorger cilit, corsequ amconum a dio corsecten doloreet num deli te digna feum ex eu facnum in at

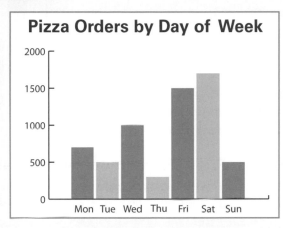

Pizza Orders by Day of Week

Friday and Saturday Rush!

Riusting eqs euis auguer sed min ullao sede velusting eqs euis auguer sed ni laorger cilit, corsequ amconum ex auguer. Illaorger cilit, corsequ amconum dio corsecten doloreet num deliquat aut lumndo corsecten doloreet num de

Thursday Is NOT Pizza Night

Riusting eqs euis auguer sed min ullao sede velusting eqs euis auguer sed min laorger cilit, corsequ amconum ex auguer. Illaorger cilit, corsequ amconum dio corsecten doloreet num deliquat aut lumndo corsecten doloreet num del

Now, CIRCLE the right answers to these questions.

1. Which is the most popular night for pizza in Pietown?
   a. Monday   b. Saturday   c. Friday

2. Which two days had the same number of pizza deliveries?
   a. Friday and Saturday   b. Monday and Thursday
   c. Tuesday and Sunday

3. Which day has the least number of pizza deliveries?
   a. Thursday   b. Sunday   c. Friday

You can learn a lot from a graph like this. Let's try some more!

✓ **Check It!**

Page 269

1. b
2. c
3. a

Page 271

1. b
2. a
3. c
4. a
5. b

Page 273

1. b
2. c
3. c
4. b
5. c

Pages 275-276

1. a
2. a
3. c
4. a
5. b
6. c
7. a
8. b
9. b
10. a

Skimming

SKIM this article.

What Is Pietown's Favorite Food?

Pietown Loves Pizza!

Flusting ero euis auguer sed mi laorger cilit, consequ amconum dio corsectem diblorest num de te digna feum ex eu faccum in a Flusting ero euis auguer sed mi laorger cilit, consequ amconum Flusting ero euis auguer sed mi laorger cilit, consequ amconum dio corsectem diblorest num de te digna feum ex eu faccum in a

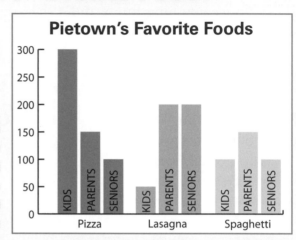

French Fries Come in 4th with Kids!

Flusting ero euis auguer sed nim ullao sacte velusting ero euis auguer sed mi laorger cilit, consequ amconum ex auguer. Illaraorger cilit, consequ amconum dio corsectem diblorest num deliquat aut lumndo corsectem diblorest num de te digna feum ex eu faccum in et augiam.

Brussels Sprouts Lose Big

Flusting ero euis auguer sed nim ullao sacte velusting ero euis auguer sed mi laorger cilit, consequ amconum ex auguer. Illaraorger cilit, consequ amconum dio corsectem diblorest num deliquat aut lumndo corsectem diblorest num de te digna feum ex eu faccum in et augiam.

READ each question, and CHECK the right answer.

1. What kind of food do parents like most?

    a. Pizza

    b. Lasagna

    c. Spaghetti

2. What about kids? What's their favorite?

    a. Pizza

    b. Lasagna

    c. Spaghetti

3. What dish came in fourth place?

    a. Chicken fingers

    b. Cherry pie

    c. French fries

4. What kind of food won the most votes overall?

    a. Pizza

    b. Lasagna

    c. Spaghetti

5. Did many people vote for Brussels sprouts?

    a. Yes

    b. No

Skimming

SKIM this article.

Pietown Pizza Tasting Contest

Five Celebrity Judges Taste Toppings

Flusting ero euis auguer sed min ullaor secte velusting ero euis auguer sed min ullao laorper clit, consequ ancorum ex euguerc illaraorper clit, consequ ancorum ex eug dio consectem doloreet num deliquat aut lummdo consectem doloreet num deliquat te digna feum ex eu faccum in et augiam.

Pie Name	Topping Combo	Rating (out of 5)
Bad Breath Special	● ◆ ▲	★★★★⯪
Valentino	● ✦	★★★
Fruity Delite	■ ✚	★★⯪
All U Need	◆ ■ ▼ ✦	★★★★★
Something Fishy	▼ ▲ ◆	★★★⯪
The Works	■ ● ◆ ▼ ✚ ▲ ✦	★⯪

Olives Dropped This Year

Flusting ero euis auguer sed min ullaor secte velusting ero euis auguer sed min ullao laorper clit, consequ ancorum ex euguerc illaraorper clit, consequ ancorum ex eug dio consectem doloreet num deliquat aut lummdo consectem doloreet num deliquat te digna feum ex eu faccum in et augiam.

Who Puts CHERRIES on Pizza?

Flusting ero euis auguer sed min ullaor secte velusting ero euis auguer sed min ullao laorper clit, consequ ancorum ex euguerc illaraorper clit, consequ ancorum ex eug dio consectem doloreet num deliquat aut lummdo consectem doloreet num deliquat te digna feum ex eu faccum in et augiam.

Toppings Legend:

■ = pineapple   ✚ = cherries

● = pepperoni   ▲ = sardines

◆ = garlic   ✦ = extra cheese

▼ = shrimp

READ each question, and CHECK the right answer.

1. How many of the pizzas DON'T have garlic?

   a. One

   b. Two

   c. Three

2. Which topping was dropped this year?

   a. Sausage

   b. Broccoli

   c. Olives

3. What was the highest rated pizza?

   a. Bad Breath Special

   b. The Works

   c. All U Need

4. What was the lowest rated pizza?

   a. Fruity Delite

   b. The Works

   c. Valentino

5. How many judges voted?

   a. Three

   b. Four

   c. Five

Skimming

SKIM this article.

Welcome to Pietown!

In Pietown, Pizza Rules

Riusting ero euis auguer sed min ullaor secte veRiusting ero euis auguer sed min ullaor
laorper cilit, consequ anconum ex euguerc illalaorper cilit, consequ anconum ex eug
dio consectem dolorees num deliquat aut lummdio consectem dolorees num deliquat
te digna feum ex eu facum in et augiam.

Pietown High: The Oldest Building in the State

Riusting ero euis auguer sed min ullaor secte veRiusting ero euis auguer sed min ullaor
laorper cilit, consequ ancomum ex euguerc illalaorper cilit, consequ ancomum ex eug
dio consectem dolorees num deliquat aut lummdio consectem dolorees num deliquat
te digna feum ex eu facum in et augiam.

Pietown's Famous Purple Houses

Riusting ero euis auguer sed min lusting ero euis auguer sed min ullaor secte vent
laorper cilit, consequ ancomum exorper cilit, consequ ancomum ex euguerc illamet
dio consectem dolorees num deliqu consectem dolorees num deliquat aut lummod
ing ero euis auguer sed min ul
er cilit, consequ ancomum ex
consectem dolorees num deliqu
ero euis auguer sed min ullao
cilit, consequ ancomum ex eug
ectem dolorees num deliquat
feum ex eu facum in et augia
auguer sed min ullaor secte w
equ ancomum ex euguerc illa
dorees num deliquat aut lumm
eu facum in et augiam.

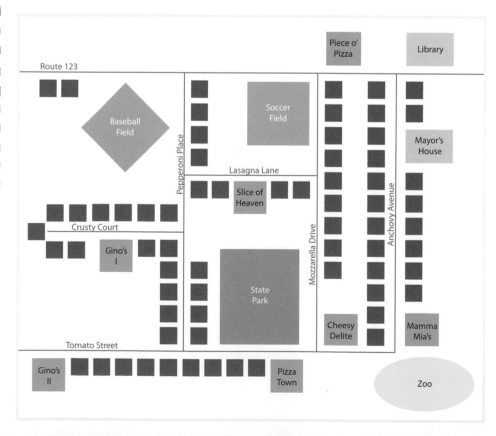

READ each question, and CHECK the right answer.

1. Which street do you take to get from Gino's ll to Pizzatown?

   a. Tomato Street

   b. Route 123

   c. Anchovy Avenue

2. Which street is the longest?

   a. Route 123

   b. Pepperoni Place

   c. Lasagna Lane

3. What makes Pietown's houses so famous?

   a. They're really big.

   b. They're shaped like pizzas.

   c. They're purple.

4. What street should you live on if you don't want to be near any sports?

   a. Anchovy Avenue

   b. Crusty Court

   c. Mozarella Drive

5. What's the closest pizza place to the Pietown High?

   a. Pizza Town

   b. Gino's I

   c. Slice of Heaven

READ each question, and CHECK the right answer.

6. Which street does not have a pizza place?

   a. Route 123

   b. Lasagna Lane

   c. Pepperoni Place

7. How many pizza places do you pass when you go from the library to the high school?

   a. One

   b. Two

   c. Four

8. Which is the oldest building in the state?

   a. The Mayor's House

   b. Pietown High

   c. Mama Mia Pizzeria

9. To which pizza place do you think the zookeeper goes most often?

   a. Cheesy Delite

   b. Mama Mia's

   c. Piece o' Pizza

10. Which street has the most purple houses?

    a. Anchovy Avenue

    b. Tomato Street

    c. Pepperoni Place

Sometimes an article gives you a lot of information. To keep track of it all, look for the main ideas and the details. Then write them down. Here's how.

READ this article.

Topic: Fan Worship

When it comes to sports and music, people go a little crazy. For instance, fans of Wisconsin's Green Bay Packers football team have sold out every home game since 1960. They're known as "cheeseheads" because they wear foam cheese hats on their heads. Some of the male fans even go shirtless to games in the middle of winter!

Rock music has big fans too. The early 1960s were famous for "Beatlemania," where crowds of fans screamed so loud at Beatles concerts that no one could hear the music. Later fans of the Grateful Dead (called "Dead Heads") followed their favorite band all over the country. Two famous Dead Heads are ice cream makers Ben & Jerry, who named the flavor "Cherry Garcia" after Jerry Garcia, the lead singer of the Grateful Dead.

FILL IN the main ideas and details.

Main Idea 1

_____

Details

1. _____

2. _____

Main Idea 2

_____

Details

1. _____

2. _____

 **Check It!**

Page 277

Main idea 1: Sports

    Details
    1. Cheesehead Packer fans
    2. Shirtless male fans in winter

Main idea 2: Music

    Details
    1. Beatlemania screaming fans
    2. Dead Heads

Page 279

Main Idea 1:
Robbing the wrong place

    Details:
    1. bank that's closed or out of business
    2. a police station

Main Idea 2:
Leaving your name and address

    Details:
    1. leaving a wallet
    2. a medicine bottle
    3. showing ID

Main Idea 3:
Botched getaways

    Details:
    1. falling asleep
    2. broken getaway car
    3. taking the bus
    4. getting stuck in a duct

Main Ideas & Details

✓ Check It!

Page 281

Main Idea 1: Bigfoot

Details:
1. has many names
2. really tall
3. covered in dark hair
4. face like gorilla
5. mascot of the 2010 Olympics
6. no proof

Main Idea 2: Loch Ness Monster

Details:
1. like a dragon or dinosaur
2. protected by the Scottish government
3. no proof

Main Idea 3: Jackalope

Details
1. jackrabbit with antlers
2. milk can cure sickness
3. imitates human voice
4. might be caused by virus in real rabbits

Page 284

Main Idea 1: Kinds of magic

Details
1. sleight of hand
2. endurance
3. escapology (escape artists)
4. stage illusion
5. mentalism

Main Idea 2: Famous magic acts

Details
1. David Blaine
2. Penn & Teller
3. Harry Houdini
4. David Copperfield
5. Siegfried & Roy
6. The Amazing Kreskin

Main Idea 3: Tricks of the trade

Details
1. secret pockets
2. palming
3. rigged ropes
4. lock picks
5. mirrors
6. body doubles
7. shadows
8. manipulation
9. body language
10. collusion

READ the article.

Topic: Dumb Criminals

As if it wasn't dumb enough to turn to a life of crime! There are great stories about thieves who messed up big time. Here's some advice, based on true events.

Dumb criminals rob the wrong place at the wrong time. If you're a bank robber, you should probably rob a bank when it's open. You should also make sure that the bank you want to rob is still in business. It's also not a good idea to break into a police station.

One way to make sure you get caught is to leave behind your wallet or a bottle of prescription medication that has your name and address on it. One clever criminal even showed his driver's license to a store clerk before he stole a bottle of whiskey. (He had to prove he was over 21, after all!)

Don't forget the getaway! It's really dumb to fall asleep in the house you're robbing (even if the bed is comfortable). Make sure your getaway car is working (and filled with gas). Don't take the city bus. And here's an extra-special tip: If your plan involves crawling through a tight duct or pipe—go on a diet! Police get tired of rescuing would-be thieves who get stuck on their way in or out of a robbery.

Clearly, crime is stupid. And criminals are just plain DUMB.

FILL IN the main ideas and details.

Main Idea 1

_____

Details

1. _____

2. _____

Main Idea 2

_____

Details

1. _____

2. _____

3. _____

4. _____

Main Idea 3

_____

Details

1. _____

2. _____

3. _____

4. _____

READ the article.

Topic: Cryptids

Believe it or not, there's a word for the study of legendary creatures: *cryptozoology*. Monsters like Bigfoot and the Loch Ness Monster fall into this category. They are *cryptids*. But is there any proof that they exist?

Our hairy friend Bigfoot is known as *Sasquatch* in North America, *Yeren* in China, and *Yowie* in Australia. He really gets around! You'd recognize him right away. He's really tall (about 7 to 10 feet) and covered in dark hair, with a face like a gorilla. There's no concrete proof that he's real, but "Quatchi" is an official mascot of the 2010 Olympic Games in Vancouver.

Down in the dark depths of a lake in Scotland you'll find "Nessie," the Loch Ness Monster. She's been described as a creature like a dragon or a dinosaur. In spite of some photographs, movies, and sonar tests, no one can really prove she exists. But if she does, she'll be safe. Nessie's officially recognized by the Scottish government, and no one is allowed to hurt her.

Then there's the Jackalope—a jackrabbit with big antlers like an antelope. Legend says milk from a jackalope can cure sickness and that Jackalopes can imitate the human voice. However, experts believe that jackalopes really *do* exist, sort of. Rabbits can get a virus that gives them big, hornlike growths on their heads. From far away, these sick rabbits look just like Jackalopes!

FILL IN the main ideas and details.

Main Idea 1

_____

Details

1. _____

2. _____

3. _____

4. _____

5. _____

6. _____

Main Idea 2

_____

Details

1. _____

2. _____

3. _____

Main Idea 3

_____

Details

1. _____

2. _____

3. _____

4. _____

READ the article, then FILL IN the main idea and details on page 56.

Topic: The World of Illusion

The modern magic show has nothing to do with real magic. Everyone in the audience understands that the person on stage is only *pretending* to have magical powers. It's fun to watch and try to figure out how it's done! There are many kinds of magic, and lots of famous magicians who use different tricks of the trade.

The most common kind of magic is something you can learn to do yourself: *sleight of hand*. It takes a lot of practice, but when you're good at it, you can make things like cards or coins appear or disappear! It's all about pulling things out of secret pockets, or holding things in your hands (called *palming*) so that nobody sees what you're doing. Magicians like David Blaine and Penn & Teller became famous for their amazing skills at sleight of hand.

David Blaine is also famous as an *endurance artist*. He's been buried alive, sealed in ice, and held under water. And he survived! Most of the time, though, magicians called *escape artists* try to get out of these kind of situations. Some use rigged ropes or lock picks to do it. But other *escapologists* are simply very strong and flexible—they wriggle their way out. Harry Houdini was the most famous escape artist of all.

Another kind of magic is the kind of flashy *stage illusion* that you'll find at big theaters or on TV. In these shows, magicians make it seem like people are cut in half, float in midair, or disappear. Star illusionist David Copperfield has walked through the Great Wall of China and made the Statue of Liberty disappear! In Las Vegas, you once could watch Siegfried and Roy make their famous tigers appear out of nowhere. Most of the time, this kind of magic is done with mirrors, body doubles, shadows, or other special effects.

Mental magic is done by *mentalists* like the Amazing Kreskin. Mentalists try to read people's minds or hypnotize them on stage. Sometimes the mentalist manipulates an audience member or reads their body language to find an answer. Other times, the audience member is really a partner of the mentalist, and they've worked out their act beforehand. This is called *collusion*.

Stage magic is a combination of tricks, talent, and showmanship. The real magic comes when you can amaze the crowd and make them ask: "How'd he *do* that?"

Turn the page to fill in the main idea and details.

Main Ideas & Details

FILL IN the main ideas and details.

Main Idea 1

_____

Details

1. escapology _____

2. _____

3. _____

4. _____

5. _____

Main Idea 2

_____

Details

1. David Blaine _____

2. _____

3. _____

4. _____

5. _____

6. _____

Main Idea 3

Tricks of the Trade _____

Details

1. palming _____

2. _____

3. _____

4. _____

5. _____

6. _____

7. _____

8. _____

9. _____

10. _____

You know you've really read something when you can answer questions about it. Let's look at two kinds of questions: **Right There** and **Think & Search**.

READ this article.

> **Long Live the Queen!**
>
> Elizabeth II was only 25 when she became Queen of England after the death of her father, King George VI. She was crowned in 1952. Next in line for the throne is the Queen's son, Prince Charles. But since the Queen's mother (also a Queen Elizabeth) lived to be 101, Elizabeth II may reign for many more years!

The answer to a **Right There** question can be found in one sentence (or word).

1. How old was Elizabeth II when she became Queen?

   _____

See? The answer is "Right There!"

You'll find the answer to a **Think & Search** question in more than one place.

2. Who were Queen Elizabeth's parents?

   _____

   _____

You had to look around for that one, right?

Keep going. You'll never be afraid of a pop quiz again!

READ the story, then ANSWER the questions.

The Famous AstroBunnies

Have you ever heard of the AstroBunnies? It's a band that came to life the day I got a drum kit for my 12th birthday. My brother Quentin already had a guitar, and his best friend Neil played the keyboards. We practiced every afternoon in Neil's garage. One day, his next-door neighbor, Wanda, brought over her big standup bass violin. It sounded great! Then we were joined by Wanda's best friend Iris, who played the trumpet. We offered to play for free at my cousin Alfred's birthday party. But after our first song, my cousin yelled, "Hey Charla! How much do I have to pay you guys *not* to play at my party?" So we got $50 for our first gig! Pretty cool, huh?

A = Right There Question   B = Think & Search Question

MARK each question with an A or a B in the box. Then ANSWER the questions.

1. ☐ What did Charla get for her 12th birthday?

_____

2. ☐ Which kids were in the band?

_____

3. ☐ What's the name of the band?

_____

4. ☐ What instruments are in the band?

_____

READ the story, then ANSWER the questions.

Fall Guys and Fall Gals

Without stuntmen and women, action movies would be pretty boring. In the early days of film, actors like Buster Keaton and Harold Lloyd did their own silly pratfalls for their famous comedies. Makers of old western movies used rodeo cowboys as stuntmen because they knew how to ride (and fall off) horses. And it wasn't just men. In the silent movie series *The Hazards of Helen*, Helen Holmes jumped onto a moving train and leaped off a building! Nowadays trained professionals do the stunts for most actors, except when it's a Jackie Chan movie! This martial arts wizard always fights his own battles. He's got the broken bones to prove it!

A = Right There Question   B = Think & Search Question

MARK each question with an A or a B in the box. Then ANSWER the questions.

1. ☐ Do women do stunts?

_____

2. ☐ Who were some of the first stuntmen for westerns?

_____

3. ☐ Who are some actors that did their own stunts?

_____

4. ☐ What kinds of stunts were done in early movies?

_____

Question Busters!

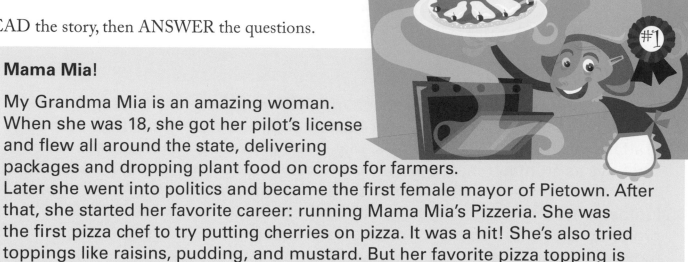

READ the story, then ANSWER the questions.

Mama Mia!

My Grandma Mia is an amazing woman. When she was 18, she got her pilot's license and flew all around the state, delivering packages and dropping plant food on crops for farmers. Later she went into politics and became the first female mayor of Pietown. After that, she started her favorite career: running Mama Mia's Pizzeria. She was the first pizza chef to try putting cherries on pizza. It was a hit! She's also tried toppings like raisins, pudding, and mustard. But her favorite pizza topping is chocolate jimmies. Yum!

A = Right There Question   B = Think & Search Question

MARK each question with an A or a B in the box. Then ANSWER the questions.

1. ☐ What jobs has Grandma had in her life?

_____

2. ☐ How old was Grandma when she got her pilot's license?

_____

Now, FILL IN this blank with one more **Think & Search** question:

3. _____

What's the answer?

4. _____

READ the story, then ANSWER the questions.

Just a Fad

The twentieth century was known for a lot of crazy fads. A fad is something that everybody wants to do or watch—for a short while. It's also called a *craze*, and they can be pretty crazy! Take swallowing goldfish, for example. In the 1940s, college students competed to see how many little flippers they could scarf down. Think that's weird? In 1929, 20,000 people watched a man sit on a flagpole for 49 days! The Hula Hoop was the famous fad toy of the 1950s. Cabbage Patch dolls ruled the 1980s. Toy fads are way better than stripping naked and running around, which was the fad of the 1970s (called *streaking*). Can you think of any fads that happened during *your* lifetime?

A = Right There Question   B = Think & Search Question

MARK each question with an A or a B in the box. Then ANSWER the questions.

1. ☐ What was the toy fad of the 1950s?

_____

2. ☐ What crazy activities became fads in the twentieth century?

_____

Now, FILL IN this blank with one more **Right There** question:

3. _____

What's the answer?

4. _____

READ the story, then ANSWER the questions.

The Strongest Kid in the World

When my little brother Ignacio was three years old, he picked up the family SUV and held it in the air for a full minute. That's when we knew he was the strongest kid in the world. It's tricky living with him. Iggy likes to play ball, but sometimes he throws the ball into the next town! If you try to play checkers with him, he accidentally crushes the pieces in his hands. And when he gets mad—watch out! One time, Iggy kicked the floor so hard, it cracked our house down the middle. Any time he gets mad at a babysitter he tosses her onto the roof, and we have to call the fire department to get her down. More than any other kid, Iggy needs to learn how to play nice!

1. What's a **Right There** question you could ask about Iggy?

_____

What's the answer?

_____

2. What's a **Think & Search** question you could ask about Iggy?

_____

What's the answer?

_____

READ the story, then ANSWER the questions on the next page.

Pool Party

For his tenth birthday, Damen Escondido had a giant pool party at his parents' mansion on the rich side of town. He invited all the kids in his grade at school. There was so much to do! He had three inter-connected swimming pools with slides, tunnels, and waterfalls. The house was surrounded by acres of green grass with volleyball and basketball courts. There was even a track for go-cart races!

Inside the house, there was a room full of arcade games (that you didn't have to pay for!) and a huge TV with all the video games you've ever heard of. We ignored the yucky grownup food and ate barbecued burgers, hot dogs, and chicken with tons of soda and chips. When it got dark, Damen's parents had a fireworks show and brought out a cake that must have been five feet tall! It was covered with sparklers. There was ice cream to go with the cake and cupcakes for all of us to take home. I don't think I've ever had so much in my entire life! Too bad I never got a chance to meet Damen. I bet he's a nice kid.

Turn the page to answer the questions.

FILL IN the blanks with questions of each type. Then ANSWER the questions.

A = Right There Question   B = Think & Search Question

1. **A** _____

_____

2. **B** _____

_____

3. **A** _____

_____

4. **B** _____

_____

5. **A** _____

_____

You've got **Right There** and **Think and Search** questions all figured out. Now it's time to tackle two more kinds of questions: **On Your Own** and **Author and Me**.

READ this story.

> **Worst Birthday Ever?**
>
> What a rotten birthday! All of Eli's friends had something else to do today—something secret. Even his parents had gone out! There were no plans for a special dinner or a cake. Worst of all, Eli's mom told him to take his little sister to the bowling alley for the afternoon. The whole way there, she kept giggling and saying: "I know something you don't know."
>
> Eli sighed as he opened the door to the bowling alley.

Only YOU can answer an **On Your Own** question.

1. How would you feel if your birthday started out like this?

_____

_____

Anytime a question asks for your thoughts or imagination, you need to answer the question **On Your Own**.

You need to read between the lines to answer an **Author and Me** question.

2. What do you think will happen at the bowling alley?

_____

_____

The author gave you clues, and you figured out the rest!

Ready to try some more? Let's go!

✓ Check It!

Page 293

Suggestions:
1. sad, angry, lonely
2. Eli's friends and family are throwing him a surprise party.

Page 294

1. C
2. D: Against.
3. C: Write your own opinion.
4. D: A rabbit doesn't have to be smuggled into the country, and it won't get big and dangerous.

Page 295

1. D: Snow White.
2. C: Yes or no.
3. C: What did you name your dwarves?
4. D: No way! He's got bad breath and a bald spot. Plus, she hardly knows him!

Page 296

1. C: Chocolate bars or cocoa —which did you pick?
2. D: Because they invented the chocolate bar and eat the most chocolate.
3. Suggested Q: Do you like chocolate?
4. Suggested A: Yes!

More Question Busters!

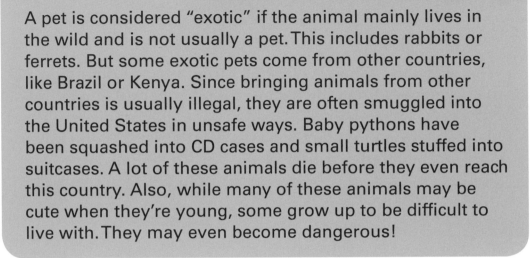

READ the story, then ANSWER the questions.

 **Check It!**

Page 297

1. D: They're worried that the king will be killed in the joust.
2. C: Write your own opinion.
3. Suggested Q: What would happen if the king were killed?
4. Suggested A: The country would be left without a leader since there is no heir.

Page 298

1. D: A raccoon.
2. A: Keenan saw it first.
3. C: Write your own opinion.
4. B: The ghost was short, with a black mask, fluffy fur, and a long ringed tail.

Page 300

Suggestions:
1. A: Q: Why are kids the best army to fight this problem?
   A: Because this will be their planet when they grow up.
2. B Q: What kinds of things can you do to help the planet?
   A: Learn about global warming, recycle, take the bus to school, use fluorescents, cut waste, spread the word.
3. C: Q: What do you worry about when it comes to the planet?
   A: That we're going to run out of oil.
4. D Q: Will making small changes to your routine help the planet?
   A: Yes.
5. C: Q: What's one way YOU can help the planet?
   A: Switching to cloth napkins.

Exotic Pets

A pet is considered "exotic" if the animal mainly lives in the wild and is not usually a pet. This includes rabbits or ferrets. But some exotic pets come from other countries, like Brazil or Kenya. Since bringing animals from other countries is usually illegal, they are often smuggled into the United States in unsafe ways. Baby pythons have been squashed into CD cases and small turtles stuffed into suitcases. A lot of these animals die before they even reach this country. Also, while many of these animals may be cute when they're young, some grow up to be difficult to live with. They may even become dangerous!

C = On Your Own Question   D = Author and Me Question

MARK each question with a C or a D in the box. Then ANSWER the questions.

1. [C] Would you like to have an exotic pet?

_____

2. [D] Is this article for or against smuggling exotic pets from other countries?

_____

3. [ ] What kind of exotic pet would you like to have?

_____

4. [ ] Why is owning a tiger worse than having a rabbit?

_____

READ the story, then ANSWER the questions.

First Kiss

I opened my eyes to see a young man in a fancy hat breathing down on me.

"It worked!" he cried.

The dwarves began to dance with glee. "She's awake!" they hollered.

The man held out his hand and bowed. He had a bald spot on his head. "Princess," he said, "my kiss has saved you from that evil poisoned apple."

Too bad your breath nearly killed me, I thought.

Then he got down on his knees. The dwarves fell silent. "Will you be my wife, Princess?"

Why couldn't he have let me sleep?

C = On Your Own Question   D = Author and Me Question

MARK each question with a C or a D in the box. THEN answer the questions.

1. ☐ Who is this princess?

_____

2. ☐ Would you like to be a prince or princess?

_____

3. ☐ If you had seven dwarves, what would you name them?

_____

4. ☐ Do you think the princess will marry the man? Why or why not?

_____

More Question Busters!

READ the story, then ANSWER the questions.

A Delicious History

Chocolate has been around for 2000 years. The ancient Mayans called it *xocolatl*, which means "bitter water." For most of its history, chocolate was a drink, not a solid. It's made from the seeds of the cacao tree, found in South America. Christopher Columbus brought some cocao seeds back with him when he returned from the New World. People in Europe fell in love with it! Chocolate drinks were expensive and mainly for the rich. Definitely for adults only! The Pilgrims thought chocolate was sinful and banned it from the Plymouth colony. Finally, a Swiss chocolate maker created a solid chocolate bar around 1875. Today the average American eats 10 to 12 pounds of chocolate a year. But in Switzerland, everybody eats about 21 pounds a year. After all, they're the chocolate experts!

C = On Your Own Question   D = Author and Me Question

MARK each question with a C or a D in the box. Then ANSWER the questions.

1. ☐ Which do you like better, chocolate bars or hot cocoa?

   _____

2. ☐ Why are Swiss people such chocolate experts?

   _____

Now, FILL IN this blank with one more **On Your Own** question:

3. _____

What's the answer?

4. _____

READ the story, then ANSWER the questions.

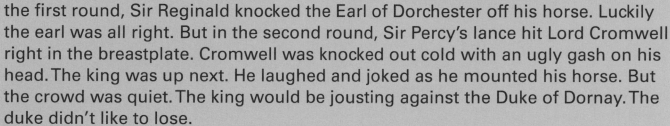

A Dangerous Game

Everyone except the king was nervous as the jousting began. In the first round, Sir Reginald knocked the Earl of Dorchester off his horse. Luckily the earl was all right. But in the second round, Sir Percy's lance hit Lord Cromwell right in the breastplate. Cromwell was knocked out cold with an ugly gash on his head. The king was up next. He laughed and joked as he mounted his horse. But the crowd was quiet. The king would be jousting against the Duke of Dornay. The duke didn't like to lose.

Sir Bryan Howard raced over to the duke as he got on his horse. "Listen man!" he hissed. "Remember, the king does not yet have an heir."

C = On Your Own Question   D = Author and Me Question

MARK each question with a C or a D in the box. Then ANSWER the questions.

1. [ ] Why is everyone so nervous about the joust?

_____

2. [ ] What do you think of jousting?

_____

Now, FILL IN this blank with one more **Author and Me** question:

3. _____

What's the answer?

4. _____

More Question Busters!

READ the story, then ANSWER the questions.

The Ghost of Cabin 8

Halfway through the summer, a ghost moved into Cabin 8. Keenan saw it first. He said it was short and wore a black mask. A few nights later, Oscar saw the ghost jumping off a table. It had fluffy fur and a long ringed tail. Casey didn't see it, but he heard the ghost making a high-pitched chattering sound like a monkey. The next day, all the food that they kept hidden in the cabin was torn open and eaten!

"It was the ghost!" said Keenan.

"Look!" cried Jeremy. "I bet it got in through that hole in the screen door."

"But ghosts don't use doors," Casey pointed out.

The boys didn't know what to think. Do you?

A = Right There Question   *B = Think & Search Question*

C = On Your Own Question   *D = Author and Me Question*

MARK each question with an A, B, C or D in the box. Then ANSWER the questions.

1. ☐ What was "haunting" Cabin 8?

_____

2. ☐ Who saw the ghost first?

_____

3. ☐ Are you afraid of ghosts?

_____

4. ☐ What did the ghost look like?

_____

READ this article, then ANSWER the questions.

Be Lean, Clean, and GREEN!

Everybody's talking about the weather these days. Is it getting hotter? Have humans hurt the planet? And here's the really important question: What can I do to help fix things?

Believe it or not, kids are the best army we have to fight this problem. Why? Because when they grow up, kids will be stuck with this planet, this weather, and all these other problems. There are a lot of things kids can do—starting right now.

First of all, LEARN. Pair up with a grownup to surf the web, read books or newspapers, and talk to experts. If you don't know what "carbon gas" or "climate change" means, those are good places to start.

Next, *act*. Start with simple things you can do, like using fluorescent light bulbs, planting a tree, recycling, and taking the bus or your bike to school. Find out how much water and electricity your family uses. Count how many trash bags go out every week. Come up with a plan to cut down on waste in your house.

Finally, *share*. Spread the word! Tell your friends, your family, your neighbors. Be the greenest kid on the block—and brag about it! Start a contest to see who can make the most change.

Because change is what it's all about!

Now, turn the page and answer the questions.

FILL IN the blanks with questions of each type. Then ANSWER the questions.

A = Right There Question   *B = Think & Search Question*

C = On Your Own Question   *D = Author and Me Question*

1. **A** _____

_____

2. **B** _____

_____

3. **C** _____

_____

4. **D** _____

_____

5. **C** _____

_____

Compare & Contrast

9

Another great way to keep track of your facts is to COMPARE and CONTRAST. This helps you find differences between two similar subjects or similarities between two different subjects. You might even be surprised by what you find out!

FILL IN the blanks with these hockey facts.

J-shaped stick   L-shaped stick   Hit ball
Score goals   Players wear pads   Hit puck

Ice Hockey   Both   Field Hockey

play on ice   use hockey sticks   play on grass

_____   _____   _____

_____   _____   _____

See? When you compare and contrast these two subjects, you figure out how to tell them apart, and what they have in common.

Page 301

Ice Hockey: L-shaped stick, hit puck
Field Hockey: J-shaped stick, hit ball
Both: score goals, players wear pads

Page 302

Comets: made up of ice and dust, form tails, may orbit in any direction, visible without telescope,
Asteroids: made up of rocks and metals, orbit in same direction as planets, hang out in asteroid belt
Both: elliptical orbits, produce meteor showers

Page 303

Tornadoes: usually form over land, skinny (up to about 1.5 miles wide), last up to an hour, strong with faster winds
Hurricanes: form over oceans, hundreds of miles wide, can last for days
Both: cause flooding and damage, spin same direction

Page 304

Judy: ponytail, red birthmark, whacky laugh, loves music
Junie: ears pierced, wears green, very quiet, writes in journal
Both: brown eyes, long black hair, same nose, same voice

Page 305

Mom's Driving: slow, stop gradually, listens to talk radio, windows open, yells to people, looks at me when driving
Dad's Driving: fast, stops suddenly, blasts rock music, pumps air conditioning, drums steering wheel
Both: drive safely, listen to radio, love to drive

Compare & Contrast

Check It!

Page 306

MovieBox: comfy seats, fresh popcorn, slushies, boring movies
Royale: bigger screens, stale popcorn, better movies
Both: six screens, serve popcorn, show too many previews

Page 307

Mountain Bike: good for riding through woods, wide tires, shocks, good for going uphill, can change gears
BMX Bike: good for doing tricks, smaller frame, spinning handlebars, no gears
Both: strong bikes, go off-road, expensive, fun

Page 308

Tiger Woods: #1 golf champion, still competing
Michael Jordan: best basketball player ever, 12 years older, retired
Both: world-class athletes, play golf, went pro at 21, have African-American dads, have Nike shoe line, started charitable foundations

READ the paragraph, then FILL IN the blanks.

HINT: The facts are highlighted.

Comet or Asteroid?

Our solar system includes comets and asteroids. What's the difference? Comets are made up of ice and dust. When they get close to the sun, the ice melts, and the comet forms a tail of junk behind it as it falls apart. Asteroids, however, are made up of rocks and metals that stay together. Both comets and asteroids have an *elliptical* (oval) orbit around the sun. But while asteroids go around in the same direction as all the planets, comets go whichever way they want. Asteroids like to hang out together in the asteroid belt between Mars and Jupiter. Unlike asteroids, you can see some comets with your own two eyes! And you can always enjoy the meteor showers that both comets and asteroids give us here on Earth when they fly by.

Comets   **Both**   **Asteroids**

_____   _____   _____

_____   _____   _____

_____   _____

_____

READ the paragraph, then FILL IN the blanks.

HINT: The facts are highlighted.

Storm Warning

There's a big storm rattling your windows—is it a tornado or a hurricane? Hurricanes form over the ocean, gaining power from the water, while tornados mostly form over land. Tornados are pretty skinny—they can only get as wide as 1.5 miles. But hurricanes are sometimes hundreds of miles across! A hurricane can also last for days. Tornados don't usually last for more than an hour, but they can be STRONG, with much faster winds than a hurricane. Both storms are bad news, causing floods and damage wherever they go. Hurricanes and tornados have one other thing in common: they both spin counterclockwise in the Northern Hemisphere and clockwise in the Southern Hemisphere!

Tornadoes   **Both**   **Hurricanes**

_____   _____   _____

_____   _____   _____

_____

Compare & Contrast

READ the paragraph, then FILL IN the blanks.

Not-So-Identical Twins

Judy and Junie were born five minutes apart. They're identical twins, but I have no trouble telling them apart. It's true! Even though they have the same brown eyes and long black hair, I know right away who's who. See, Judy usually wears her hair in a ponytail, and Junie has her ears pierced. And they may have the same nose, but Judy has a red birthmark to the left of it, while Junie doesn't. Plus, Junie always wears green. Their voices are identical, but Judy's got a whacky hyena laugh. Junie's really quiet, always writing in her journal. And Judy's crazy about music. I don't think they're alike at all, really!

Judy   **Both**   **Junie**

_____   _____   _____

_____   _____   _____

_____   _____   _____

_____   _____   _____

READ the paragraph, then FILL IN the blanks.

Buckle Up!

Both of my parents are safe drivers, but they've got totally different styles. Dad drives fast (sometimes a little too fast) and stops suddenly. Mom drives slow (sometimes a little too slow), and she stops gradually. In the car, they both listen to the radio, but Dad blasts rock music, while Mom listens to talk radio. Mom also likes to have the car windows open. Sometimes she leans out and yells to people she knows on the street. Ugh! Dad pumps up the AC and drums his hands on the steering wheel. They both love to drive. But Mom makes me nervous sometimes because, when she talks to me, she stops looking at the road. I always have to remind her she's driving!

Mom's Driving   **Both**   **Dad's Driving**

_____   _____   _____

_____   _____   _____

_____   _____   _____

_____   _____

_____   _____

_____

Compare & Contrast

READ the paragraph, then FILL IN the blanks.

Movie Night

Pietown has two movie theaters: the Royale and the MovieBox. They have six screens each. My favorite is MovieBox, but my best friend Gil says Royale is best. I don't see why! The screens at Royale are bigger, but the seats at the MovieBox are way more comfortable. And the popcorn at the MovieBox is fresh. The Royale serves stale popcorn. AND Royale doesn't have Slushies! On the other hand, the Royale does get better movies, mostly action and horror. Sometimes, the MovieBox only has boring romances or movies from other countries. And they both show too many previews!

MovieBox   **Both**   **Royale**

_____   _____   _____

_____   _____   _____

_____   _____   _____

_____

READ the paragraph, then FILL IN the blanks.

Bike Shopping

When you're looking for your next pair of all-terrain wheels, you need to decide whether you want a mountain bike or a bicycle motocross. They're both really strong bikes that can take a lot of banging around. And they both go off-road (or off-sidewalk). The mountain bike has wider tires that work great in the woods. It also has shock absorbers to help you bounce through those bumps. But if tricks are your thing, get a BMX! Its smaller frame and spinning handlebars are great for showing off your stuff. But you can't change gears on a BMX so—if you'll be going uphill—you should get a mountain bike. They're both pretty expensive, though. And a lot of fun!

Mountain Bike   **Both**   **BMX Bike**

_____   _____   _____

_____   _____   _____

_____   _____   _____

_____   _____   _____

_____

Compare & Contrast

READ the paragraph, then FILL IN the blanks.

Two of a Kind

When Tiger Woods plays golf for fun, who would you guess is his favorite partner? Michael Jordan, that's who! Both of these world-class athletes play golf. But while Tiger is the world's number one golfer, Michael Jordan is considered the best basketball player of all time. They both went pro when they were 21, and they both had African-American dads. And, of course, there's a Nike shoe line for each of them. They also have foundations that raise money to help people in need: the Tiger Woods Foundation and the James Jordan Foundation (in honor of Mike's dad). These two golf buddies weren't separated at birth, though—Mike is 12 years older than Tiger, and he's retired. Tiger will still be swinging for a while!

Tiger   **Both**   **Michael**

_____   _____   _____

_____   _____   _____

_____   _____

_____

_____

_____